Lafite

By the same author

The Gourmet's Companion (Edited with introduction)
The Compleat Imbiber (Edited annually since 1956)
The Wines of Italy
Morton Shand's A Book of French Wines (Revised and edited)
In a Glass Lightly

Château **Lafite**, the main façade with mediaeval tower and the
seventeenth-century terrace

Lafite

The Story of Château Lafite-Rothschild

Cyril Ray

STEIN AND DAY/*Publishers*/New York

First published in the United States of America in 1969 by Stein and Day/*Publishers*

Copyright © 1968 by Cyril Ray
Library of Congress Catalog Card No. 69-17938
All rights reserved

Printed in the United States of America

Stein and Day/*Publishers*/7 East 48 Street, New York, N.Y. 10017

To

my son
JONATHAN
for whom
I have laid down some
LAFITE

CONTENTS

ILLUSTRATIONS

Illustrations

NOTE: With the exception of the coroneted monogram on page 68 which is taken from the mourning stationery of the Baroness Betty, the chapter-headings and other decorative drawings in the text are from *La Vigne: Voyage Autour des Vins de France* by Bertall. The sub-title of this sizeable work—'Etude Physiologique, Anecdotique, Historique, Humoristique et Même Scientifique'—gives an idea both of its wide range and of its gossipy but informative, sometimes facetious, sometimes agreeably ironic, quality. It was published (in Paris) in 1878, but Bertall was gathering his material in the Médoc in 1876: the drawings here give a very good idea of how Lafite, its people, its visitors, and its surroundings, must have looked at the time of the Rothschild purchase, only eight years earlier.

Lafite

Introduction

I DO not know when I first tasted Lafite, or what vintage it was that I first drank. It may well have been years ago that I poured it down, unknowing and uncaring, and it may well have been one of the noblest years of that noblest of growths, for I had hospitable friends with well-stocked cellars long before I had acquired a taste of my own or a proper respect for what I was drinking. A journalist, in any case, dines frequently above his station, at city banquets and public celebrations; it may be that as a reporter in the nineteen-thirties I drank vintages of Lafite and of other classic growths that I ought now to be boasting about.

But I have never kept a diary of my eatings and my drinkings: it was too late in life that I came upon the truth that if you keep a diary, one day it will keep you.

What I do know about Lafite, though, is that I first visited the château, already a devoted admirer of its product, for I had been a writer about wine some half-a-dozen years, in the June of 1962, to help to celebrate the Fête de la Fleur, the flowering of the vine, as the Médocains do every year, in great style, and also to be proclaimed a Commander du Bontemps du Médoc et des Graves, the chief investiture of which is held each year, to coincide with the fête, in a different château of the region. In 1962, it was the turn of Lafite; my sponsor was M. Guy Schÿler, who is a brother-in-law of a kind friend of mine in Champagne, Mme Odette Pol Roger, and who acts as host at Château Lafite on Baron Elie de Rothschild's behalf; and the wine that we had to taste, supposedly identify, and pronounce upon, as part of the initiatory rites, was the 1961 Lafite.

I write 'supposedly identify', because behind us all, in our newly-donned claret-coloured and fur-trimmed velvet robes of the fraternity, our sponsors were hissing at us what the wine was lest, in trying to give it a name, we disgrace ourselves and them— and if the word 'Lafite' does not lend itself much to hissing, its year 1961 does, whether in English or in French—so that all we had to do was to mime our dubieties as convincingly as we could before coming out proudly with what we claimed to be our conclusions.

From each neophyte there had to be a speech of sorts, comic or otherwise, and before it came to my turn I had realized that only facetiousness would distract attention from my fractured French. I opined, therefore, as the microphone came my way, that the wine was red; that no doubt it was French; that it might well be Médoc; that it was conceivably even Pauillac; that—who knew?—it might well even be Lafite. If so and, as seemed likely, it was the 1961, the one thing I *was* sure about, I said, was that it was too dear for the likes of me.

Only that very morning, it had been announced in the local press, and volubly discussed by the day's concourse of visitors to the château, that the Lafite 1961 had just fetched the highest price ever paid for a French red wine, and my wry jest raised a similarly wry laugh from those Bordeaux *négociants* and those wine-growing rivals of Lafite—well represented, as a matter of tradition, at a Fête de la Fleur celebration and a Bontemps investiture—who could understand my French.

But my little joke, such as it was, failed to amuse Baron Elie de Rothschild, administrator and part owner of Lafite, whom I found lying in wait for me on my way from the platform in the park to the splendid luncheon that had been spread for us in the *chai*: oh, so I thought his wine was too dear, did I?

No use protesting that it had been just a joke; that it had raised the facile laugh that had been all that I had intended; that in light-hearted speeches of this sort—and in a foreign language, at that —a man was not on oath. Baron Elie insisted that I bear in mind that no wine was made with greater care; that the price paid only yesterday, and reported that very morning, demonstrated clearly that no claret was more sought after; that a single-crop farmer— which was what a wine-grower was, after all—had to take his good prices when he could: there were all too many ruinous years.

I duly made the points that—as I was being obliged to be serious—I felt should be made. Chiefly that, although I sympathized with everything that Baron Elie had said, I could not help feeling that he was pricing out of the market for the finest clarets the one class that for three hundred years had not only supported the claret trade but, because this class was articulate, and its members wrote and talked about wine, had made claret's world-wide reputation: the lettered English middle class. Not the rich, not the noble, but schoolmasters and country solicitors, doctors and dons. And deserting them, so to speak, in favour of the ficklest wine-drinkers in the world—the rich Americans. Folk who would undoubtedly drink Lafite this year because its record price had been widely discussed, but who next year might drink only Berncasteler Doktor, as they had done in the year that Dr Adenauer made a much-publicized present of it to President Eisenhower, and in the year after that drink only Taittinger Blanc de Blancs, because it had been given the dubious accolade of a mention in a James Bond novel.

I could have said then, as I could write now, much more. So could Baron Elie. Indeed, whenever he and I have met since then the argument has continued, and is still unresolved. But sure as I had already been that this, for me, at any rate, was the greatest of all red wines, (and red wines give me more frequent pleasure than do white), I had now learned something of the care with which it was made and the fierce pride with which it was sold, as well as having made the acquaintance of one of the prettiest châteaux in the Médoc, and been told something of its history. So that when, some years later, a publisher suggested that I should break new ground by writing not about wine in general, or even a type of wine, but about one wine in particular, about the place it was made, and the people who made it, the first name that sprang to my lips was not, as it might once have been (and as it might be, I hope, on some other, future occasion), Schloss Johannisberg or Château d'Yquem, but Château Lafite. And all the more appropriately because there seemed a chance to bring out such a book just after the centenary year of its purchase by Baron Elie's great-grandfather, Baron James, whose widow it was who furnished the house with the damasks and the Daguerro-types, the grained woodwork and the story-telling woolwork that still reflect the last enchantments of the Second Empire.

* * *

3

As it turned out, this book has been written under difficulties that I could not then have foreseen. Many of the Lafite records were burned by members of the staff there after the Rothschilds had gone and just before the Germans moved into the house in 1940; they were over-zealous, for there is every reason to believe that the documents would have been respected; the wines in the cellar were. Then, throughout most of the period during which the book was being written, the bank at 21 Rue Laffitte, head-quarters of the French Rothschild empire, was in process of being extended and rebuilt: I was told of boxes of papers that might prove to be relevant, but nobody knew just at the moment where they were, and nobody had time to look for them or, should they turn up, to sort them out. Some such papers did, in fact, suddenly make their appearance within a matter of a week or so only of my manuscript having to be in the publisher's hands: they have been studied more cursorily than scholarship demands, and there is much scope for some future writer about Lafite who will, I hope, be able to deploy more scholarship than I command. In particular, there is material that may provide new and surprising facts about methods of vinification in the mid-nineteenth century.

To my delight, though, enough material came my way, and with just enough time to spare, to shed light on what had been obscure up to the very last moment about the ownership of Lafite before the Rothschilds bought it: I had spent a disproportionate amount of time on the problem; letters to the trade press and to the archivists of English banks and of French *départements* had yielded nothing, and I had even found myself facing an official letter from Paris apologizing for the fact that one file that might have contained a document to resolve my questions had been destroyed by the *communards* of 1871.

Worst of all, just after I had settled down to what I intended to be a serious, concentrated period of work on the material I had gathered and was still gathering, my own house in Kent was struck by lightning and completely destroyed.

So, from the very beginning of my work on this book I have had no settled place to do it in; I had lost sheets of preliminary notes, and had to turn elsewhere, and to more places than one, to verify the references that in the ordinary way would have needed no more than the stretch of an arm towards my own collection of books on wine in general and on the Médoc in particular.

Fortunately, I was able to spend virtually a couple of months—four weeks in the summer and three during the vintage in October—at Lafite itself. For the rest of the time I have carried cardboard boxes of books, papers and rough first drafts of my own manuscript from the country to London and back again; from one borrowed cottage to another; from a London attic bed-sitting-room to a club library; from one club library to another; and from club to the remotest underground recesses of the London Library—farther even than the place sacred to the files of *The Times*, and as far as the shelves that bear the volumes of the *Illustrated London News* for the 1850s.

I mention all this not to excite sympathy, but to explain any shortcomings in scholarship and in style. But if this little book should prove readable at all, and of any value, then there are those to be thanked who made my task easier than it might otherwise have been, or encouraged me when—I must confess—it seemed to be beyond me.

First of all, of course, the Baron and Baroness Elie de Rothschild. The baron gave me carte blanche to come and go at Lafite and to take up my residence there when it suited me. The Baroness showed the greatest possible interest in the book from the beginning; entertained me at her house in Paris and on her visits to Lafite; and patiently answered endless questions about the château, its pictures and its furnishings, and about the family, both by letter and over the luncheon table.

But I owe it to the Baron and the Baroness, to my publisher, and to myself to make it quite clear that this is in no way a *sponsored* book. It was commissioned by the publisher in the ordinary way of business, and it is in the ordinary way of business that it is being published. Nobody at the Rothschild bank or at Lafite has had any say—save when I have asked for specific information on matters of fact—in what I should or should not write. Nobody at the Rothschild bank or at Lafite has paid me a fee. All the opinions expressed are my own, and some of them are not shared by the Rothschilds or by those at Lafite.

M. Georges Nemes, Directeur-Général des Domaines Rothschild, whose headquarters are in Paris, and under whose jurisdiction Lafite falls, along with so much other bank and family property, has been hospitable as well as helpful, as also has M. Guy Schÿler, whom I have already mentioned as my sponsor at the Bontemps, and who was my frequent host at Lafite and in Bordeaux.

M. André Portet, the *régisseur* at Lafite, together with his heads of departments and some of his other workers, among whom I lived for many quiet and happy weeks, are mentioned in the following chapters. I hope I have made it clear there that this book could not have been written without their help. But I must make especial mention of M. Portet's son, Jean-Pierre, a most helpful interpreter, and of Mme Germaine Petit, wife of the Lafite gardener, who cooked my meals for me for weeks on end (I had Lafite with everything), and washed my shirts as well.

At other times during my stay in the Médoc I was entertained by Mr and Mrs Ronald Barton at Château Langoa-Barton and by Mr and Mrs Peter Sichel at Château d'Angludet. They were all helpful in my enquiries, as well as hospitable, and on both these grounds I owe a very special debt to the Baron and Baroness Philippe de Rothschild at Château Mouton-Rothschild. Few know as much about the making and the marketing of the finest clarets as Baron Philippe, and nobody could have been more magnanimous in helping a stranger who was engaged on a book about his closest rival.

In the same breath, as it were, and for similar reasons, I should like to make especial mention of Mr Steven Schneider of Cambridge, Mass., and a partner in the Bordeaux firm of William Bolter & Co., of Bordeaux. Throughout the period during which I was working on this book, Mr Schneider—poet, scholar and wine-shipper—was heavily engaged, and I understand still is, on a most detailed history of the *crus classés* of the Médoc. He was extremely understanding about my difficulties and positively lavish in sharing the results of his own painstaking and scholarly researches. I have experienced American generosity before, and have long admired American scholarship: it was a most agreeable and rewarding experience to meet these qualities in so helpful a combination.

M. Jean-Bernard Lion, of the legal department of the Rothschild bank in Paris, finally solved for me the problem of who owned Lafite before the Rothschilds and how it came to be for sale in 1868. M. Jacques Vialard, *notaire* at Pauillac, like his father and his grandfather before him (and, curiously enough, a direct descendant of a family—the Gombauds—who owned Lafite before even the eighteenth-century Ségurs), took me patiently through the legal intricacies of the ownership of Lafite during the war and under the German occupation. More light was thrown for me on this period by Mme Gaby Faux, now living in retirement at Le Pouyalet, who was book-keeper at Lafite from 1920 to 1951 (having succeeded her grandfather, who held the same position from 1871 to 1920), and virtually the Rothschild's unofficial custodian while the Germans were in the château.

Mlle Yvonne Meyrand of Libourne helped me at Lafite with various French books and documents, as did M. Guy Schyler. My friends at British United Airways were as courteous and helpful as ever in getting me and my car to and from France: this is the third book that they have helped me to write.

For help in research, my thanks are due to Mrs Joan St George Saunders, of Writer's and Speaker's Research. Mr Michael Broadbent, M.W., of Christie's, and Mr Colin Fenton, M.W., of Harvey's of Bristol, have been generous with their tasting notes and other information, and Mr Edmund Penning-Rowsell, the wine correspondent of the *Financial Times*, has been a source of constant encouragement and help. I am indebted, too, to Sir Guy Salisbury-Jones and to Mr David Peppercorn, M.W.

Mr Robert Jay Misch in New York, Mr Alan Bell Macdonald in Edinburgh, and Mr Tom Whelehan in Dublin have been indefatigable in ferreting out, or in trying to ferret out, rare vintages of Lafite in the restaurants of their respective cities. Finally, and especially, I must thank my friend and publisher, Mr Derek Priestley, of Peter Davies, for a far greater continued interest and, indeed, enthusiasm than an author has a right to expect.

*   *   *

Some words about words. The French word *vignoble* and the English word 'vineyard' are both used in rather vague and general senses and, although their meanings overlap, they do not coincide.

To the French, a *vignoble* is any wine-growing area. The whole of the five-hundred-square-mile area around Bordeaux that is planted with vines is a *vignoble*; so is each of the districts that compose it—the Médoc, St Emilion, the Sauternais, Entre Deux Mers, and so on. So is each commune in each of these districts, such as Pauillac, a commune of the Médoc, and so is *the wine-growing part* of each of the estates in the commune.

Thus, the whole estate of Château Lafite is *not* a *vignoble*, because it includes marsh and meadow and woodland; it is the *domaine*, or the *propriété*: the *vignoble* of Château Lafite is made up only of those forty *parcelles* (or *pièces*) that are planted with vines. Each of these, incidentally, has its proper name, like the meadows of an English farm, and this is how it is referred to in the day-to-day conduct of affairs: La Fosse, or Les Hantes, or Mamizelle.[1]

In English, we should call not only the whole of the Château Lafite property a vineyard (in distinguishing between a 'single-vineyard' wine—that of Lafite—and a commune or a district wine, entitled only to the name Pauillac or Médoc, and blended from the wines of many properties) but also each *parcelle* goes by that name, in that we should say that at Lafite such a vineyard is planted with Cabernet Sauvignon, and another with Merlot; such a one faces east, or another is better drained.

In this book, I have tried to avoid ambiguity by referring to what the French would call the Lafite *vignoble* as Lafite, simply, and to its individual *parcelles* as 'vineyards'. But it must be remembered that (with two very small outlying exceptions) these

[1] There is a sort of Domesday Book at Lafite, with a page for each individual *parcelle* and a plan to each page, drawn to scale, recording how many rows of vines it is planted with, covering what area; how much area is taken up with paths; what species of vines they are, and when they were planted; what is the composition of the soil and how well or how badly it drains; when it has suffered from what diseases; how many casks it has produced in each year—a book so detailed as to show which parts of a one-acre field are gravelly, which clayey, and which sandy, and whether it is less or more liable to spring frosts than its neighbours.

vineyards form a compact whole, and that the forty *parcelles* produce what we should call a single-vineyard wine: Lafite.

Then, *cépage*, which means any single variety of vine—Cabernet Sauvignon, say, or Merlot—and *encépagement*, which is a property's particular blend and proportion of vines. Thus, the *encépagement* at Lafite is two-thirds of the *cépage* Cabernet Sauvignon, one-sixth each of the *cépages* Merlot and Cabernet Franc.

To avoid confusion, I have tried to use the word *encépagement* only in this latter sense, referring otherwise to a 'vine', or a 'variety', or using the proper name. Indeed, I have tried to use French words as little as possible, and only where they make the meaning simpler, and where English would confuse.

* * *

Then, the Rothschild titles. All the five original Rothschild brothers were made barons of the old Austro-Hungarian Empire in 1822: the titles devolved on the members of the English branch as on the others, though they do not use them. The French Rothschilds are also barons of the Second Empire. The French and the Austrian patents of nobility, unlike an English peerage, bestow upon all male members of the family the title of 'baron', and the French Rothschilds use it, as well as the particle, '*de*'.

Baron Elie is the younger son of a younger son, and if the title were English, like his cousin Lord Rothschild's, he would be a plain mister. But in France he is Baron Elie de Rothschild, and to everyone at Lafite, which he governs, he is 'Baron Elie', and it is thus that he must be referred to here. His wife, Liliane, is '*La Baronne*' at Lafite, and in these pages she is referred to as the Baroness.

The widow of the Baron James de Rothschild who bought Lafite is referred to here as the Baroness Betty, which is how the family speaks of her.

* * *

Château Lafite's name derives from an old French word meaning a height, or modest eminence. Until well within living memory it has been spelled variously with two 'fs' and one 't'; one 'f' and two 't's; with two of each; and with one of each. In each of the various quotations given in this book I have retained the author's spelling, but the correct modern usage is as given here, whereas the address of the Rothschild bank in Paris is Rue Laffitte.

*   *   *

Finally, let me say that it was never intended that this should be a technical book about viticulture or vinification. It is about Lafite, not about how to make Lafite. I have tried to give a sketch, simply, of the cycle of the year in the vineyards and of the processes in the *chai*. For greater detail, I commend the serious student to the late Allan Sichel's *The Penguin Book of Wines*, London 1965, to which I have myself turned for greater clarification and systemization of what I have learned in vineyard and in *chai*. Other books to which I have referred are listed in the bibliography.

1. The Médoc

OF the vineyard that is France, the richest corner is the south west.

One square mile in ten of the five thousand square miles of the *département* of the Gironde, of which the great city of Bordeaux is the centre and the capital, is under vines. Each year, these five hundred square miles of vineyards produce around one-tenth of all the wines of France—one-fortieth of the wine of the world.

What is of greater importance still—for the Midi produces even more, but of poorer quality,—is that two-thirds of this total from the Gironde is of high enough quality to attain the status of wines with *appellations controlées*: wines, that is, of which the names are recognized and protected by French law, so long as their producers continue to observe, and are seen to observe, all the restrictions that the law imposes—restrictions as to the type of vines they come from (the grapes that are recognized are the so-called 'noble' grapes of France) and the density at which they are planted; the kind of soil they are planted in; the way they are pruned; the amount of wine produced from each hectare; the methods of vinification; the alcoholic content of the finished wine; and much else.

The Institut National des Appellations d'Origines des Vins et Eaux-de-Vie (I.N.A.O.) lays down the basic principles for these *appellations*, which are adapted to each region by experts on local needs and customs. The Ministry of Agriculture gives the restrictions the force of law, and there are inspectors to see that they are obeyed. The smaller the area to which an *appellation* is granted, the stricter the requirements, the finer the wine, and the greater the pride of the grower in the name. Thus, Château Lafite would be entitled to style itself 'Bordeaux: *appellation controlée*' but, finer still, it is 'Médoc'. Finer again, because more restricted, is 'Haut Médoc', and within the *appellation* 'Haut Médoc' is the most restricted of these, as it were, concentric circles: the *appellation* granted to the commune, Pauillac, within which Lafite lies, and the name of which it bears on its label. Beyond that, as single châteaux in the Médoc do not have individual *appellations* of their own, the château can apply only its own standards. A wine could fail to come up to the standard that Lafite sets for itself, and still be entitled to the *appellation* 'Pauillac' and there are years when Lafite does *déclasser* some of its wine, and sell it as 'Pauillac', simply.

The Gironde produces between one-third and two-fifths of this A.C. (*Appellation d'Origine Controlée*) wine of France, from the great luscious white dessert wines of Sauternes and Barsac, grown in the pretty wooded country that stretches thirty miles or so up the Garonne from Bordeaux, to the full red wines of Pomerol and of the postcard-picturesque little medieval city of St Emilion, on the other side of the Dordogne; and from the light, semi-sweet white wines of Entre Deux Mers—the land between the rivers, which is to say the Dordogne and the Garonne —by way of the finer whites and reds of the Graves, around Bordeaux itself, to the reds of Bourg and of Blaye, east of the Gironde, the wide, tidal river, running north into the Atlantic from Bordeaux, that is formed by the meeting of the Garonne and the Dordogne.

Here, though, we are concerned with one particular estate growing one particular wine in one specifically delimited district of the whole region—a commune entitled to the *appellation* Pauillac within the area given the *appellation* 'Haut Médoc', a narrow strip of land that lies along the left bank of the Gironde, north of Bordeaux, as far as just beyond the village of St Estéphe, about thirty-five miles from Bordeaux.[1]

The Médoc itself is the triangular peninsula that consists largely of the northern stretch of the great pine forest of the Landes, its clearings, and a string of coastal lagoons—a countryside, reaching as far again to the south, from the base of the triangle almost to Bayonne, once of creeping sand-dunes and barren marsh, through which the shepherds had to stalk their flocks on stilts, and gradually reclaimed from Colbert's time until just before the Revolution, but more skilfully and intensively during the Second Empire and the Third Republic, by afforestation and drainage.

Along the eastern edge of this peninsula of the Médoc, though, by the shore of the Gironde, lies a strip, never more than about a dozen miles wide, and often much less, of softer and more varied country.

The villages throughout the Médoc are small and drab, but where there are gardens or window-boxes or, just as likely, plants in old petrol tins, there are hollyhocks and hydrangeas and geraniums, seldom anything more exotic. Occasionally, a melancholy little palm tree struggles to bear witness, as its kindred do at Torquay and Dun Laoghaire, to what the locals would like the visitor to marvel at as a sub-tropical climate, but the creeper on the walls is wistaria or a climbing rose, never a bougain-villaea.

It can be hot in the Médoc in the summer, hotter than in England: it usually is: hot and humid. And it can be raw and dank in the winter. But, again, the weather is Atlantic, not Mediterra-nean and, as Mr Cyril Connolly has written,[2] the climate of the

[1] The Médoc used to be divided into 'Haut Médoc' and 'Bas Médoc', the former being higher up the Gironde, which is to say the southern part of the region, the latter being downstream, or to the north. During the Second World War, the people of the Bas Médoc successfully appealed to have the 'Bas' deleted, so that the name 'Médoc' now applies to the whole region or, in the matter of wine *appellation*, to the downstream part of it, formerly Bas Médoc, the twenty-three communes of which produce wines that are sound, but inferior to those of the twenty-nine communes of the Haut Médoc, which retains its name.

[2] In a magazine article reprinted in his *Ideas and Places*, London 1953.

Médoc is, 'as near perfection as a temperate maritime climate can be . . . it is southern England removed to the furthest point south at which it would remain both green and industrious'.

The pine forest and dunes of the Landes protect the eastern strip of which I write from severe westerly gales, but often enough westerly and north-westerly winds sweep cloud upon cloud into the wide Médocain sky. I have known hot days of blue, unclouded sky here, but few such succeed each other without a break, whether of rain or of heavy overcast. And though the Gironde here may be, as Mr Connolly assures us it is, 'a noble stream, like the Mississippi at New Orleans', I have never seen it, not even under the bluest of blue unclouded skies, anything other than a surly grey or a bilious brown.

Oak, ash, elm and chestnut are the trees here, not pines, so that the landscape has more of a familiar look to English eyes than the dark forest of the Landes. Bordeaux is in the latitude of Parma—south, that is, of Venice, the valley of the Po, and some of the great wine-growing regions of Italy;—but this is a cisalpine and an Atlantic, not a Mediterranean countryside, with a maritime climate, so that the landscape is green, and there are briars and bramble in the hedgerows; clover and cow-parsley in the verges; daisy and dandelion; nettles and vetch.

Many glimpses one has of this eastern Médoc—from one's motor-car as one drives northwards out of Bordeaux or, from some café table, framed at the end of a village street—look very much like the Weald of Kent: a smooth curve of pasture; a copse of bosomy deciduous trees; grey water beyond; a sky that is soft grey near the horizon; with cumulus clouds, white against the higher blue, that repeat the curves of woodland and meadow. It is only as the motor-car moves on, or as one leaves the café table to turn the corner of the village street, that one catches sight of the shallow pitch of the pink-tiled roofs, and reminds oneself: this is the south.

The vineyards, interspersed here with pasture and market-garden and copse, with a few pine-woods straggling in from the west, are not so evocative of the south as the tiled roofs, for there are vineyards in Champagne and Alsace and Germany that are little farther south than the Weald, but they are reminders, all the same, that this above all, this eastern strip of the Médoc, is wine-growing country.

Here—and there are even some dedicated burgundy-lovers who will accept this, for they agree that there are more great clarets than there are great burgundies: they argue only as to which are the greatest—here grow most of the greatest red wines in the world. And for those who (as a rule: there are special occasions) prefer not only reds to whites, dry to sweet, still to sparkling, natural to fortified, but clarets to even the greatest of burgundies—here grow the greatest wines in the world, without qualification.

2. The Wine of the Country

For three hundred years—from the marriage in 1152 of Eleanor of Aquitaine to Henry of Anjou (soon to be King Henry II of England) until the fall of Bordeaux in 1453—the Médoc, as part of the duchy of Aquitaine, was in obedience to successive kings of England, and the French chroniclers of the time frequently referred to Gascons as 'Englishmen'.

This English presence in France was the cause of constant warfare, as the *bastides* of the region bear witness—fortified towns, designed as refuges for the countryfolk of the district, and easily defensible.

So the boundaries of the duchy, under French pressure, were constantly changing, the curious thing being that the part of the duchy on which the English grip never loosened until the very end was Bordeaux and its immediate surroundings—the claret country, although the wines of the Médoc itself were not of much importance at this time.

It is only in the English-speaking countries that the red wine of Bordeaux is known generically as 'claret', though the word drives from the French '*clairet*', which has now quite a different connotation in France, meaning a light red, or deep rosé wine made to be drunk young. But the word was being used in England, however indiscriminately, (and however unlike the claret of the time was from the claret we know now,) certainly in the fourteenth century, if not earlier, when 'in any normal year', according to an article by Mr J. L. Kirby in *History Today* (January 1968), 'more than two hundred ships left Bordeaux after the harvest laden with wine for English ports, carrying perhaps 13,000 tons or four-fifths of the annual English consumption. In return, Bordeaux imported cloth, fish and corn, largely from England, though partly from Flanders and northern Europe.'

Not only cloth, fish and corn. I have been told, or I have read somewhere, that there are village churches around Bordeaux built of Bath stone, brought back as ballast in the Bordeaux ships that had taken wine to Bristol. And one cannot fail to observe, when one is in the region, the fondness of the Bordelais for Dutch cheese, whether imported or a French-made simulacrum of the real thing—an odd thing to find in a country that makes hundreds of cheeses, every one of them more interesting than Edam or Gouda, but a traditional regional taste that goes back to that same claret-fleet's coming back with round, hard, long-lasting cheeses as ballast, whether from Holland itself or from an English port that shipped cheese from abroad as well as wine.

In the period of which we write—that of English rule in Aquitaine—the wine shipped from Bordeaux was drunk young— *de l'année*—and it was those areas nearest to the city that were the best-known, and the wines of which were the most highly-prized, both at home and abroad: the wines of St Emilion, of Blaye and, especially, of Graves.

Indeed, the Médoc as a wine-growing area seems to have become sizeable and serious only towards the end of the sixteenth and the beginning of the seventeenth century, largely owing to the improved methods of viticulture introduced by Olivier de Serres and the encouragement of Henri IV, when vines were planted extensively in reclaimed marshland, and in areas previously under wheat or maize.

Reclaimed marshland is not the likeliest soil in which to grow fine wine, and it must have taken some time, in any case, even for those vines planted in the more suitable gravelly slopes of the district to produce wine as good as that of the older-established vineyards nearest to Bordeaux on the other side of the city, and across the river.

Meanwhile, throughout the eighteenth century, such Médoc wines as came to England were classed with, but considered inferior to, those of the Graves. It is significant that the first known mention in English literature of a named single-vineyard claret was of a Graves, in Samuel Pepys's entry in his diary for April 10, 1663: '. . . to the Royall Oak Tavern in Lumbard Street, where Alexander Broome the poet was, a merry and witty man, I believe, if he be not a little conceited, and here drank a sort of French wine, called Ho Bryan, that hath a good and most particular taste that I never met with'.

Another English name for claret in those days was 'Pontac'. The *Oxford English Dictionary* defines this as, 'a sweet wine obtained from Pontac, in the Basses Pyrenées, in the south of France', but Pontacq (near Jurançon) is the place-name referred to, whereas Pontac was the name of the great Bordelais family that in those days owned Haut Brion and other vineyards. I believe the O.E.D. here to be wrong, and that in the seventeenth century and much of the eighteenth 'Pontac' meant, to the English, Bordeaux wines in general; more particularly the red wines of the Graves; sometimes the wine of Château Haut Brion itself, and sometimes its second wine. (Though it was later extended to a red wine of the Cape, as people today might talk of 'South African claret'.)

One of the O.E.D.'s own quotations for the word is from Mandeville's *Fable of the Bees* (1714): 'Those that cannot purchase true hermitage or pontack, will be glad of more ordinary French claret', which does not suggest a sweet wine from the Pyrenees, and in 1683, only twenty years after his fellow-diarist's reference to 'Ho Bryan', John Evelyn wrote of having met M. Pontac, 'the son of the famous Bordeaux President, owner of that excellent *vignoble* of *Pontaque* and Obrien, whence the choicest of our Burdeaux wines come'.

So, too, John Locke, in the same period, wrote of the *vin de Pontac*, as being, 'so much esteemed in England', and as coming from, 'Mr Pontac's near Bordeaux'.

This was a time, though, of rapid change—in the development of the great vineyards of the Médoc, (now that their vines were well-established, and the superiority of the gravel slopes over the reclaimed marshland recognized,) as producing wines more elegant and more subtle in their appeal than the bolder wines of St Emilion and the Graves, and in the growth of their prestige among claret-lovers both in France and—more particularly—in England.

As early as 1707, an advertisement in the *London Gazette* announced the sale of 'an entire Parcel of New French Claret ... being of the Growth of Lafitt, Margouze, and La Tour ...'[1] Sir Robert Walpole (1676–1745) bought named growths of the Médoc, which were shipped to him direct. Dr J. H. Plumb has quoted[2] from the Walpole account books that have survived, those of 1732 and 1733, (though Walpole was buying wine long before this), purchases of four hogsheads of Château Margaux at a time, and a hogshead of Lafite regularly every three months, the only other named claret in the accounts being Pontac, which was already cheaper than the Médocs.

It is noticeable, by the way, that the Methuen Treaty of 1703 did not result in so drastic a replacement of French wines by Portuguese as is often supposed: Walpole was buying port *before* the Methuen Treaty, but he continued, after it, to buy plenty of claret, which he clearly preferred.

Both M. André Simon and Warner Allen have pointed out that there was nothing revolutionary in the preference guaranteed by the Methuen Treaty, which provided that in return for the admission of British woollens into Portugal, Portuguese wines should pay one-third less duty than French. The Portuguese had, in fact, been enjoying a *higher* preference than this since 1697: all that the treaty of 1703 did was to give international sanction to what for some years past had been the *minimum* preference.

Dr Plumb shows very clearly that in spite of rising prices, the high-born went on drinking claret throughout the early

[1] A very early singling-out of what were to become the 'first growths' of the Médoc. See Chapter 3.

[2] In *Men and Places*, London 1963.

eighteenth century: port was the drink of the smaller sort of country squires—perhaps because they were more generally Whigs, loyal to the Hanoverian succession, and glad to turn their backs on claret, with which Tories with Jacobite leanings drank to 'the king over the water'—who was in the country, in fact, where claret came from. And perhaps the country squires could not afford claret so easily as the nobler sort, such as Walpole, himself a Whig, but with Tory tastes and the money to indulge them.

The Médoc wines became highly regarded among English connoisseurs, in spite of their having to pay, like all French wines, so much more duty than those of Portugal, long before they acquired a similar prestige in France itself.

We have seen that Walpole was importing wines from the Médoc during the first decades of the century; so was the Prince of Wales who was to become George II; so, too, also in the 1720s and 1730s, was James Brydges, Duke of Chandos.

Whereas it seems not to have been until some years after 1755, when the Duc de Richelieu, great-nephew of the Cardinal, victor over the British at Fontenoy and at Port Mahon, became Governor of Guyenne and Gascony, holding almost regal court at Bordeaux (and indulging, apparently tirelessly, in every sort of sexual excess), that claret began to compete for court favour with the burgundy that Louis XIV had loved, and with the still and (more recently) the sparkling wines of Champagne that were the favourites of Louis XV.

The story has it that the sixty-year-old Richelieu had been prescribed by his Bordeaux physician the wine of Lafite as a tonic, and that when he next visited Versailles he was complimented by Louis XV on looking twenty-five years younger than when he had been appointed to his governorship.

'I must tell your Majesty', he replied, 'that I have discovered the secret of eternal youth:[3] the wine of Château Lafite', some of which he presented to the king. According to Denise Bourdet, the Pompadour gave it at her supper parties, and the Du Barry would

[3] Richelieu married for the third time at eighty-four, and died at ninety-two.

drink nothing else.[4] The story is quoted in almost everything written about Lafite, but I have found no serious source for it. There is another story, for what it is worth, quoted by M. Alexis Lichine, to the effect that Richelieu arrived in Bordeaux so dedicated to burgundy that he could be made to taste claret only by giving him a bottle with a faked label. Perhaps in those days there was no difference in the shape of the bottle, though I doubt this.

However all this may be, it is certain that it was at about this time that claret became a courtly wine in France, with the Médocs at their head; it seems highly probable that Richelieu had something to do with this change in taste, for it coincided with his appointment to Bordeaux, he was a *bon vivant*, and he was much at court. It may even be that it was Lafite in particular that he introduced there: we have seen that it had long been regarded in London as one of the greatest of clarets.

* * *

But it was not the claret we know today.

At that time, and for some decades to come, the wine of the Médoc, if it was not to be drunk *de l'année*, or if it was to be exported, was frequently blended with the coarser wines of the south.

Thus, Henderson wrote in 1824 that the red wines of the Bordelais 'are too often subjected to various processes by the merchants of Bordeaux, with the view of preparing and adapting them for particular markets . . . there is even a particular manufacture, called *travail à l'Anglaise*, which consists in adding to each hogshead of Bordeaux three or four gallons of Alicante or Benicarlo, half a gallon of stum wine,[5] and sometimes a small quantity of Hermitage. This mixture undergoes a slight degree of fermentation; and, when the whole is sufficiently fretted in, it is exported under the name of CLARET.'

[4] If there is substance in this statement, then it is agreeably appropriate that the enchanting Vigée-Lebrun seated portrait of Madame Du Barry should have the place of honour in the small Louis Seize salon at Baron and Baroness Elie de Rothschild's eighteenth-century Paris house in the Rue Masseran, where there is also a Sèvres table service that once belonged to the Du Barry.

[5] Alicante and Benicarlo are both Spanish wines: 'stum' is unfermented grape-juice.

Henderson went on to say that this was true only of *vin ordinaire* or the secondary growths of the Médoc, 'for the prime growths fall far short of the demand which prevails for these wines', citing Lafite, Latour and Château Margaux as being beyond reproach.

Yet M. André Simon records having seen an invoice of the early 1830s from one of the most highly respected wine-merchants of Leith for some 'Lafite Hermitaged'. He writes that, 'there was no vintage mentioned, and the wine may have been that of a poor year, or a blend of two indifferent vintages, which had been "improved" by the addition of a good, stout, red Hermitage. There was no deception.'

And it is clear from letters written in the 1850s to his principals by Goudal, the *régisseur* at Lafite, that for a good deal longer— well into the middle of the century and pretty well up to the Rothschild purchase of the property in 1868 (if not longer)—the poorer vintages of even that noble growth were *hermitagé*: strengthened in flavour and in alcohol, and deepened in colour, by the addition of wine from the southern Rhône valley.

Burgundy was similarly treated—as its lesser wines are to this day by the addition of wines from North Africa, Corsica and the Midi, to make *vins ordinaires* sold under brand names. No harm is done if there is no hoisting of false colours. Warner Allen recorded in his *A History of Wine* that he was told by a most eminent burgundy shipper that in his (the shipper's) grandfather's time 'practically the whole yield of Hermitage and Châteauneuf-du-Pape was destined to give colour, alcohol and body to feebler wines grown elsewhere, Hermitage being ear-marked for Bordeaux, Châteauneuf for Burgundy'.

It is reasonable to assume, as both claret and burgundy were fortified in similar ways, that although each of them differs from the wine as we know it today, their positions relative to each other must have been much the same as they are now—claret the lighter and more delicate, more refreshingly balanced between fruit and acidity; burgundy bigger and blander; the one feminine in its grace, the other masculine in its strength: the queen and the king, respectively, of red wines.

This, of course, when each wine is at its most typical. Vintages differ, and not every wine runs true to form. There are clarets that always, there are clarets that sometimes, approximate to burgundy in style, just as there are burgundies that are lighter and more delicate than one expects.

And the range of clarets is so wide that there are considerable differences between them, arising from the *encèpagement* of each— the proportion, that is, of different breeds of grape;—from minor variations of climate, soil and drainage of the vineyards; from different views about picking late and picking early; and from different methods of vinification.

Very generally speaking, the wines of the Médoc are more delicate and yet longer-lived than those of St Emilion and Pomerol, rather crisper and more definite in flavour and in fragrance than those of the Graves.

Then there are differences within the Médoc itself.

It would be very roughly true to say that the fine wines of this region, in spite of their strong family resemblance, become 'bigger' in style and in body as they are produced farther and farther from Bordeaux—thus, the wines of the commune of Margaux are lighter than those of St Julien; St Julien lighter than Pauillac; Pauillac than St Estèphe.

That having been said, it must then be added that Lafite is an exception to this generalization. It lies at the northern edge of the commune of Pauillac—indeed, one or two of its outlying sections are actually in St Estèphe—between Château Mouton-Rothschild (Pauillac) and Château Cos d'Estournel (St Estèphe), which are both eminently full, rich, robust wines. Yet Lafite is just as notably a light wine, and although this quality of lightness is deliberately enhanced these days by the *encèpagement*, or proportions of the various types of vine grown there, as is explained in a later chapter, there is no doubt that slight differences of soil and sub-soil between Lafite and its neighbours have always helped to determine differences of character in their wines.

Latour is a 'bigger' wine than Lafite, and so it was in 1824, when Henderson wrote that 'the vineyard of Latour, which gives the strongest wine of Médoc, at least among the first growths, lies on a gently rising ground immediately above Pauillac. As it is nearer the river, the soil is probably richer than that of Lafitte, which produces the lightest of the choice Médoc wines.'

Mouton is also a 'bigger' wine than Lafite, and is also a next-door neighbour, and Henderson observes that 'the wine of Bran-Mouton,[6] which has a similar aspect, and is divided from Lafitte only by a narrow footpath, sells for one-third less . . . the quality of the soil appears to be somewhat stronger'.

*   *   *

We have already seen that as soon as the wines of the Médoc established themselves on the English market, Lafite was among the most highly prized of them: as early as 1723, Bruneval, wine-merchant to the then Prince of Wales (soon to be George II and, like his first minister, Walpole, a claret-lover) writing from Bordeaux, ranked Lafite, Latour, Margaux and Pontac (meaning, in this instance, Haut Brion) in that order as the leaders of their class. Between 1703 and 1725 John Hervey, first Earl of Bristol, was buying 'Lafitte' or 'La Fitte', along with 'Margoose', 'Obrian', 'Langoon' (Langoa), 'Pontack' and 'La Tour'. To come to the end of the century, there are two letters dated 1791 and 1795 from M. André Simon's collection that are now at the Maison du Vin in Bordeaux, and sometimes shown there in a display cabinet, in which the London wine-merchant advises an unnamed 'Your Lordship' of the despatch of 'Lafite claret', in one instance as much as ten dozen of it at a time.

The clarets that Captain Gronow of the Guards mentioned by name[7] as being those that he and his fellow-officers were eager to drink when they reached Bordeaux after chasing Soult across the Pyrenees were 'Larose, Lafitte and Margot', though he was wrong to suppose that they were not exported to England. (And he had to admit that 'our palates, accustomed to the stronger vintages of Spain, I suspect were not in a condition to appreciate the more delicate and refined bouquets which ought to characterize claret.' In any case, 'in the Guards, Bordeaux was more affectionately remembered in connexion with its women than its wine.')

[6] Château Mouton then belonged to Baron Brane.
[7] In his *Reminiscences*, 1862.

Clarets were usually drunk younger in those days than they are now, and were often blended with coarser wines, as we have seen, to give them body and staying power. But it is reasonable to suppose that the differences between the general styles of these leading wines were similar to what they are now: Lafite and Château Margaux both lighter and more gracious in character than Latour, which takes longer to mature, through being harder and fuller, which makes it a more satisfactory wine in poor years, when Lafite and Margaux can seem to lack body. Lighter, too, than Haut Brion, the greatest of the Graves, of which wines Warner Allen wrote[8] that, 'they are remarkable for their brilliant colour, their breed and a certain austere majesty in their *finesse* . . . they cannot quite equal the balance, the velvety smoothness and seductive bouquet of Médoc at its best . . . they are awe-inspiring rather than loveable'.

But this consistency of relative style is no mere assumption. There is evidence that the great growths did indeed differ then, even in a period of younger, coarser wines, in much the same way as they do now.

Henderson has already been quoted, seeking to find in their respective soils, a century and a half ago, an explanation for Lafite's being a lighter wine than either of its neighbours, Latour and Mouton, as it is now. And in the same book he essayed a comparison of what were already, a generation before the classification of 1855, regarded as the first growths, that would not seem far off the mark today:

'Of the RED wines of the Bordelais, the Lafitte, Latour, Château Margaux, and Haut-Brion, are so greatly esteemed, that they always sell from twenty to twenty-five per cent higher than any others of the province. The first-mentioned is the most choice and delicate, and is characterized by its silky softness on the palate, and its charming perfume, which partakes of the nature of the violet and the raspberry. The Latour has a fuller body, and, at the same time, a considerable aroma, but wants the softness of the Lafitte. The Château Margaux, on the other hand, is lighter, and possesses all the delicate qualities of the Lafitte, except that it has not quite so high a flavour. The Haut-Brion, again, has

[8] In his *Natural Red Wines*, 1951.

more spirit and body than any of the preceding, but is rough, when new, and requires to be kept six or seven years in the wood; while the others become fit for bottling in much less time.'

Cyrus Redding, in his *A History and Description of Modern Wines* (I quote from the second edition, published in 1836) wrote of Lafite, 'a wine surpassed by none of its rivals', that 'it is lighter than Château Latour and may be drank [sic] somewhat less in age', and of Latour that, 'this wine is distinguished from that of Château Lafitte by its superior body and consistence; but it should be kept in wood at least a year more than the Lafitte to attain a proper maturity. . . . It is less fine than Lafitte.'

*   *   *

The characteristics of present-day Lafite are more difficult to define than to recognize, though many have tried their hand.

Mr Frank Schoonmaker, the American shipper and writer, says of it in his *Encyclopaedia of Wine*: 'In the opinion of most impartial experts, and perhaps in the mind of the general public as well, the *ne plus ultra* of Claret . . . an astonishing authority, impeccable breeding, fruit and fragrance and depth of flavour, all the qualities with which a great Claret should be endowed.'

M. Alexis Lichine has referred, in his *Wines of France* to 'the great light wines [of Lafite], famed for their finesse', elaborating this, in his *Encyclopaedia of Wines and Spirits*, into 'great finesse and a particular softness imparted by the Merlot grape. The wine tends to be firm, yet delicate and supple, with an eventual light-ness developed in age. Lesser vintages are still excellent wines, lighter than those of great years, but always showing breed, fragrance and depth of flavour.'

Opinions differ, of course. George Saintsbury thought that 'the best Latour' was 'rather better' than Lafite, and 'a thoroughly succeeded Margaux to be quite as good', but it had to be 'the best' Latour and a 'thoroughly succeeded' Margaux, and Warner Allen pointed out that Lafite of the best years did not figure in Saintsbury's cellar-book. He was comparing the best of their kind with something not at its best.

Maurice Healy was devoted to Haut Brion, having succeeded in convincing himself, Irish of the Irish, if he convinced no one else, that it must originally have been named O'Brien. Even so, he ranked many years of Latour and (particularly) of Cheval Blanc higher than the corresponding Haut Brions, and wrote that, 'Lafite has filled my glass with wine and my heart with gratitude probably more often than any other wine'. And T. Earle Welby, though he thought Latour 'the firmest and grandest of Médocs', and Château Margaux as, 'ordinarily having more of what most people would call poetry', than Latour or Lafite, nevertheless thought the 1864 Lafite 'the best claret of the nineteenth century', and the 1874—whatever he had already credited Château Margaux 'ordinarily' as having—when he tasted it in 1919 as 'the most poetic claret I have ever had'.

Morton Shand, writing about the growths of the Médoc in *The Wines of France*, was rapturous about Château Margaux as 'the most delicate and poetic of the three' first growths, about. Latour as 'the most richly spacious and inspiring . . .', and about Mouton as 'a complete and flawless wine', but when he came to Lafite said simply that 'its flavour and bouquet are considered so grand and sublime as to afford a symposium of the virtues of all other wines'.

And although Warner Allen thought in 1951 that the Lafites of the twentieth century were not maintaining their nineteenth-century reputation (he was soon and frequently to be confounded: he had not then tasted the 1947 and the 1949, let alone guessed what was still to come), he was saying the same thing as Shand when he wrote in his *Natural Red Wines* that 'certainly no wine can equal a fine Margaux in delicate fragrance and subtlety of texture, even though Latour may surpass it in firmness and determination of appeal, [and] Lafite in that perfect balance which merges all virtues in a transcendental unity'.

'Perfect balance'. It sums it all up.

3. The Classification

P ARIS was gay in the summer of 1855.

The Second Empire was not yet three years old; the Emperor's marriage even less than that, and his lovely Empress still in her twenties. Some said that their court was flashy; it was certainly not dull.

Through the ancient slums and rookeries of the capital M. Haussmann was driving avenues and boulevards the straightness and width of which may well have been intended to make it easy for disciplined troops to mow down a revolutionary mob, but which also made crinolines more manageable. 'Paris is signally transfigured', wrote the Prince Consort that summer to his uncle Leopold of the Belgians, 'by the Rue de Rivoli, the Boulevard de Strasbourg, the completion of the Louvre, the great open square in front of the Hôtel de Ville, the completion of the Palais de Justice, the restoration of the Sainte Chapelle, and especially by the laying out of the ornamental gardens in the Bois de Boulogne . . .'

Far away, in the Crimea, the Emperor's armies, under a tough new commander-in-chief, stood poised, alongside the Queen's, for the final assault on Sebastopol, its defenders dispirited by the death of the indomitable Czar who for a time had inspired them with the feeling that they were waging a Holy War for the soil of Mother Russia. To many Parisians, it seemed that the war was as good as won, and that with this second Napoleon, styled the Third, *la gloire* had come again.

Within the besieged Crimean city was the young Tolstoy, gunner officer and apprentice to letters. But in Paris it is Jacques Offenbach who seems to us to have been the spirit of the place: at his theatre in the Champs Elysées little feet under their crinolines tapped in time to his seductively danceable airs. It was a rustling age, as Philip Guedalla wrote, of millinery and dance music.

Offenbach summed up, satirized and set to music all the gaiety and the gaudiness, the naughtiness of the visiting foreigners and the way that Paris made money out of it, when he came to compose *La Vie Parisienne*. That iridescent bubble of an *opéra bouffe* was blown in time for the Paris Exhibition of 1867, but what it reflected was the Exhibition year of 1855, when not only the Empire, but all the world, seemed young, and the Emperor, newly returned from a springtime visit to Buckingham Palace, Windsor (where the Waterloo Room had been tactfully rechristened 'the Picture Gallery'), and the as yet unstaled delights of the Crystal Palace, made ready for his hostess's return visit to a universal exhibition of his own, 'a shade more modish, a thought less improving'—to quote again Philip Guedalla—'than the gleaming monument of good intentions with which Prince Albert had obliterated Hyde Park four years before'.

Napoleon III had set up an Imperial Commission for an Exposition Universelle de Paris on Christmas Eve, 1853, a year after his proclamation as Emperor, and a month before his marriage. He appointed Prince Napoleon, his cousin and his nominated heir-presumptive, as its president.

Between that appointment and the opening of the Exhibition, Prince Napoleon had gone out to the Crimea as a major-general and come back under something of a cloud. His nickname of *Plon-Plon*, said the soldiers he had commanded at the Alma, ought to have been *craint-plomb*. But whatever his bearing on the battlefield, he was still the heir to the Empire—the Empress was not yet even pregnant—and he had a reputation, not only as a radical republican, which went ill with his station in life and a preoccupation with his own princely rank, but also for capacity and drive.

Nevertheless, the opening of the Exhibition had to be postponed from May 1, 1855, to May 10, and from May 10 to May 15.

Even then, in a brief interlude of cold, damp, wretched weather in what was to be a sunlit summer, the Prince's inaugural speech to the Emperor was a string of apologies and excuses in what the *Illustrated London News* reported as 'a wilderness of yet unopened packing cases'.

A fortnight later, the stalls and galleries were described as being 'like housemaids in the forenoon', having 'not yet had time to make themselves fit to be seen', and the complaints of both visitors and exhibitors rumbled and reverberated through the sunny days of June.

By the time, though, of the visit of Queen Victoria and Prince Albert, in August, the Exhibition was as splendid as the weather, and when, in the second week of September, the guns of the Invalides boomed out the news of victory at Sebastopol—not only decisive victory, and not merely allied victory, but specifically French victory—Paris gave itself up to gaiety and glory.

*   *   *

One of the attractions of the Exhibition was a display of Bordeaux wines, for which the commissioners had invited the Bordeaux Chamber of Commerce to set up *'une représentation complète et satisfaisante des vins du départment'*. And it is a matter of note that the *représentation* was of the wines of the Bordeaux region in general, that is to say the *département* of the Gironde, not only of the Médoc.

It was decided that the wines of the *département* should be presented by communes except for those already referred to as the *crus classés*: the classed growths, or the finest wines of the region.

The question was, which were the finest?

To decide this question—or, rather, to confirm and to coordinate and make official the various classifications that had been produced during the past century, the Chamber of Commerce, in its turn, called in the *courtiers*—the Bordeaux brokers who, as middlemen between growers and shippers, were then and are now the men who know most about the prestige and the prices of Bordeaux wines.

More specifically, the Chamber of Commerce turned to the Chamber of Brokers then attached to the Bourse de Bordeaux, a more formally constituted body than the Brokers' Syndicate of today, for they were nominated by a governmental decree.

On April 18, 1855, just before the Exhibition opened, the joint committee of members of the Chamber of Commerce and of the Chamber of Brokers presented their classification of the red and of the white wines of the Gironde, '*dont les elements ont été puisés aux meilleures sources*'.

All the wines of the Gironde were called but, with the exception of Château Haut Brion, a red Graves, none but the red wines of the Médoc and the white wines of the Sauternais was chosen.

Apart from Haut Brion, the red wines of the Graves, which throughout the Middle Ages and up to the middle of the eighteenth century had been far more highly regarded than those of the Médoc, had by now fallen far behind, in the care with which they were made and, therefore, in the esteem in which they were held and the prices they could command.

As we saw in the previous chapter, the rise to fame of the wines of the Médoc dates from early in the eighteenth century in England but in France only from about a century earlier than this 1855 classification.

But at about the same time that the Duc de Richelieu was causing the wines of Lafite to be talked about at court, communications began to be improved with the wild, thinly populated region of the Médoc, the vineyards of which lay farther away from the commercial and road centre, and port, of Bordeaux, to which it had long been easier to despatch the wines of the Graves and of Pomerol and St Emilion. Château Haut Brion is almost at the edge of the city; St Emilion and Pomerol easy of access, across the river. But Pauillac, where lie Lafite, Latour and Mouton, is thirty-odd miles away, through country that for a long time was not only difficult but dangerous.

Thus, the wines of Lafite, which in 1641 we find classified simply among the *'vins de Graves et du Médoc'*, sold only locally, because of poor communications, and at between eighty and a hundred *livres* a *tonneau*, by 1745 had reached 1,500 to 1,800 *livres*, and by the eve of the Revolution, thanks to Richelieu, Pompadour and Du Barry, a dizzy peak of 2,200 *livres* a *tonneau*.

From time to time during this period, so as to simplify their transactions, brokers and shippers had formulated 'classifications' of the great wines of the region, so that the committee of 1855 was far from working in the dark, or breaking new ground.

In addition to their own knowledge of the market of their own time, they could draw upon a century of carefully recorded and tabulated experience: it was already more than seventy years since, in 1782, the classifications that had begun to take shape in the 1750s crystallized into five grades of *crus*, or growths, each grade separated from the others by price.

So indeed it was that when, at ten in the morning precisely, on the fifteenth of Fructidor, in the year V of the French Republic, one and indivisible (July 15, 1797), that same republic put up for auction the Domaine du Lafite, the previous proprietor of which had lost his head on the guillotine three years earlier, Lafite could already be described as *'premier cru du Médoc, et produisant le premier vin de Bordeaux'*.[1]

Earlier even than that, François-de-Paule Latapie, Inspector of Manufactures, reporting in 1785 to the royal Council of Commerce on conditions in the Généralité of Bordeaux, praising the red wines of the Graves, singled out one only by name, Château Haut Brion, as being 'sold at the same price as those of the other *grands crus* of the Bordelais, Lafitte, Latour and Château Margaux'.

So, too, William Franck, writing in 1824, refers to the wines of Château Haut Brion as ranking with the *'trois premiers crus du Médoc'*, which he mentions elsewhere as being Lafitte [*sic*], Latour and Margaux, quoting the list made some years previously by A. Jullien, and based on the prices obtaining since 1782. Jullien gave châteaux Margaux, Laffitte [*sic*] and Latour in that order, as the Médoc's first growths, and headed his list of second growths, with Château Brane-Mouton, as it then was, followed by Château

[1] As is dealt with more fully in Chapter 4.

Rauzan. A list of 1827 in the possession of Mr Ronald Barton of Léoville and Langoa follows precisely up to this point, but then places Léoville after Rauzan, where the 1824 list prefers Lascombes.

Also in 1824, the English writer Henderson, in his *The History of Ancient and Modern Wines*, refers to first and other 'growths'; states that 'of the red wines of the Bordelais, the Lafitte, Latour, Château Margaux[2] and Haut Brion, are so greatly esteemed, that they always sell from twenty to twenty-five per cent higher than any others of the province'; and begins his listing of the prices then recently obtainable in Bordeaux thus:

RED Médoc Wines		1815	1818	1822
		Francs	Francs	Francs
Lafitte Château Margaux Latour	The tun of 821 litres, or 217 gallons	3100	3300	3300
Rauzan Durfort Lascombe Léoville Larose Branne-Mouton[3]		2300	2500	—

Cocks, writing in 1846, refers to 'classed wines' as being 'distinguished by the denomination of first, second, third, and fourth *crus*, or growths', and also makes it clear that the differences between them are a matter of price:

'classification of growths is the order of merit assigned to wines. It has been established by custom, according to an estimate determined by trade. In forming, therefore, the following lists, I have not only had recourse to whatever has already been written

[2] Always referred to as *Château* Margaux so that there shall be no confusion with the simple commune wine, Margaux—a distinction unnecessary in the case of Lafite, Latour and the others, which do not share their names with their communes.

[3] The then owner of Château Mouton was Baron Brane or Branne—the name is variously spelled.

on this subject, but have availed myself of the various information afforded me by those whom I have considered the most com-
petent judges; price having appeared to me the best test of the
quality supposed to exist in each wine.'

He lists the first growths as Lafite, Château Margaux, Latour
and Haut Brion, in that order, which is the one in which they
would appear, nine years later, in the classification of 1855: he
refers to Lafite as having 'latterly sold dearer than any other wine'
(which, as we shall see, it still does), adding, though, 'without
the trade considering it better than the three other first growths.'

It is also significant, in view of what was to come, that he heads
his list of second growths with Mouton, which he refers to elsewhere, too, as 'an excellent second growth'.

It will be seen that it had already been quite firmly established
which were the first growths, and the same was true of the leading
seconds, although there were differences of opinion about the
order in which they should be placed.

There was still, in fact, a certain amount of chopping and
changing among the others—Franck refers not to a fourth and a
fifth growth, but to a fourth and a 'second fourth', while the list
that N. T. Thierry, the Bordeaux shipper, put out in 1822 began
as follows:

	Vins Rouges Médoc	*Prix du Tonneau ou 4 Barriques*		
		1821–1820	1819–1818	1815–1814
1er cru:	Haut-Brion, Château- Margaux Latour et Lafite	3200	3500–3600	—
2me cru:	Rauzan, Léoville, Larose, Mouton, Gorce	2300	2600–2700	3000–2500
3me cru:	Cantenac, Margaux, St Julien, Pouillac [*sic*] et St Estephe	1200	1600–1700	2400–2100
4me cru:	Bourgeois supérieurs des mêmes paroisses et de Labarde	600–700	900–1000	2000–1800
5me cru:	Bourgeois ordinaires des mêmes paroisses	540–600	700–750	2000–1400

—lumping commune wines into his category of 'third growth', and *bourgeois supérieurs* and *bourgeois ordinaires* into fourth and fifth growths, a method of classification that was not then usual, nor likely to commend itself to the Bordeaux Chamber of Commerce.

The Chamber's first reaction, indeed, to the request from the Commission of the 1855 Exhibition for a new classification had been that they would rather have no hand in such a thing: they proposed that they should put the wines of the region on show without any indication of *cru* or of owner, and argued that one exhibition could not in any case alter an order of merit that was already established and well known, but might well disturb a classification based on long experience.

Prince Napoleon insisted that the names of *crus* and proprietors should be indicated, according to an up-to-date table of merit, and the Chamber again produced the argument that the existing classification was already more than a century old, and that any meddling with it would be very dangerous, and against the interests of the proprietors themselves.

They attached to their memorandum a copy of a classification they regarded as already in force, established by long tradition: the list of first growths consisted of Lafitte [*sic*], Château Margaux, Latour and Haut Brion, in that order.

It was only after months of wrangling between the Chamber of Commerce, the Secretary-General of the Exhibition, and Prince Napoleon himself, in which at various times the first-growth châteaux had joined in that, as has already been recorded, the Chamber of Commerce called in the *courtiers*.

To a great extent this was a hand-washing device—the Chamber wrote to the Exhibition authorities:

'*L'ordre des noms, leur classement, sera ainsi une chose dont la responsabilité, en cas de reclamation et de plainte, retombera sur les courtiers; la Chambre est à l'abri de toute critique.*'

The Chamber need have had no fear. The brokers, basing their conclusions only partly—as will be seen—on their tastings of the samples that had been submitted, and chiefly on their own experience of current and recent prices, combined with earlier records, produced a list of first growths precisely the same as that originally submitted by the Chamber, and in precisely the same order.

Their famous list is reproduced in Plates I, II and III.

There was controversy then, and controversy still persists, over the precedence within each category.

The evidence is contradictory. A letter of September 16, 1855 from the Syndicat des Courtiers to the Chamber of Commerce stated that it had not been their intention to distinguish between the wines of each category, but to regard all as of equal merit. On the other hand, the first growths are not placed in alphabetical order, whether of the name of the property or of the owner or of the commune, and if the order is not alphabetical, then what is it?

Against the proposition that in that case the order must be accidental and arbitrary, there is the fact that this letter flatly contradicted one of August 14, only a month before, in which the Syndicat had stated that the second, third, fourth and fifth growths were placed in order of merit, pointing out that thus, according to the wish expressed by the Chamber of Commerce, Château Mouton found itself at the head of the second *crus*.

Both Château Mouton-Rothschild and Château Margaux, I know, maintain that the order of the first growths, nevertheless, and unlike that of the others, is one of pure chance. I would not wish to appear partisan about this—indeed, I do not feel partisan—but there seems to be considerable substance to Lafite's claim to be first among the firsts, and to have been placed there deliberately.

In any case, it seems unreasonable for Mouton to make much of its own position as, in the words of the Syndicat, '*en tête des seconds crus*', and patently there by merit, and neither by alphabetical order nor by chance, while denying (as there are those devoted admirers of Mouton that do) that there is any significance in Lafite's similar position at the head of the firsts.

Château Margaux has what seems at first sight a better-based grievance. There is some evidence (though there is evidence to the contrary, too: Lafite was told otherwise at the time) that after at any rate one blind tasting at the Exhibition of *such samples as*

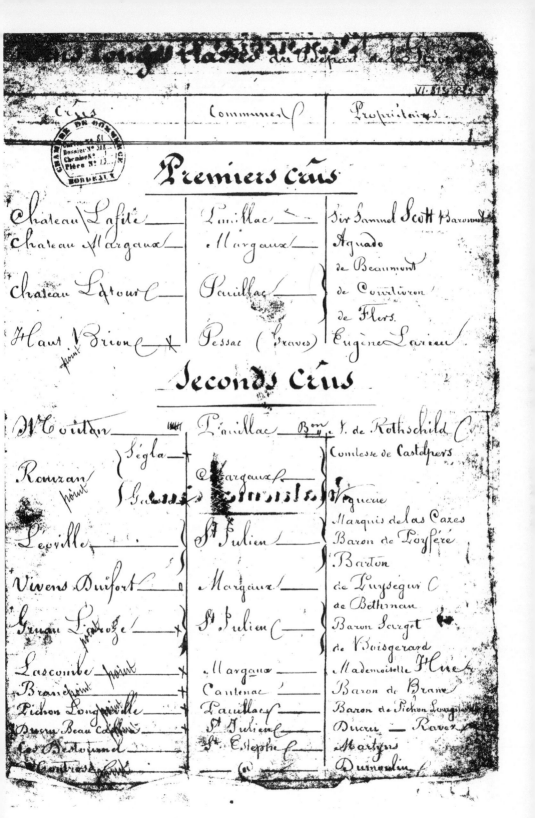

1855 Classification: First and Second Growths
(The blemishes, evident in the original document, are caused by the ink having
soaked through from one side of the sheet to the other.)

PLATE I

Troisièmes Crus

Crus	Communes	Propriétaires
Kirwan	Cantenac	Descheyver
Château d'Issan		Blanchy
Lagrange	St Julien	Comte Duchatel
Langoa	"	Barton
Giscours	Labarde	J. P. Pescatore
St Exupéry	Margaux	Fourcade
Boyd	Cantenac	Plusieurs Propriétaires
Palmer	"	Emile Pereire
Malescot	Ludon	V. Douffroy, Fiston.
Des mirail	Margaux	Sipière
Dubignon	Margaux	D. Dubignon
		M. Dubignon
Calon	St Estèphe	Sivère Lestapis de Paris
Ferrière	Margaux	V. J. Ferrière
Becker	"	Szjarderski y Rolland

Quatrièmes Crus

Crus	Communes	Propriétaires
St Pierre	St Julien	Bontemps Dubarry
		V. Roullet.
		V. Galloupeau
Talbot	"	Marquis d'Aux
Du Luc	"	Du Luc ainé
Duhart	Pauillac	Castéja
Poujet Lassalle	Cantenac	Izan
Pouget	"	de Chavaille
Carnet	St Laurent	de Luetkens
Rochet	St Estèphe	V. Lafonde Camarsac

1855 Classification: Third and Fourth Growths

PLATE II

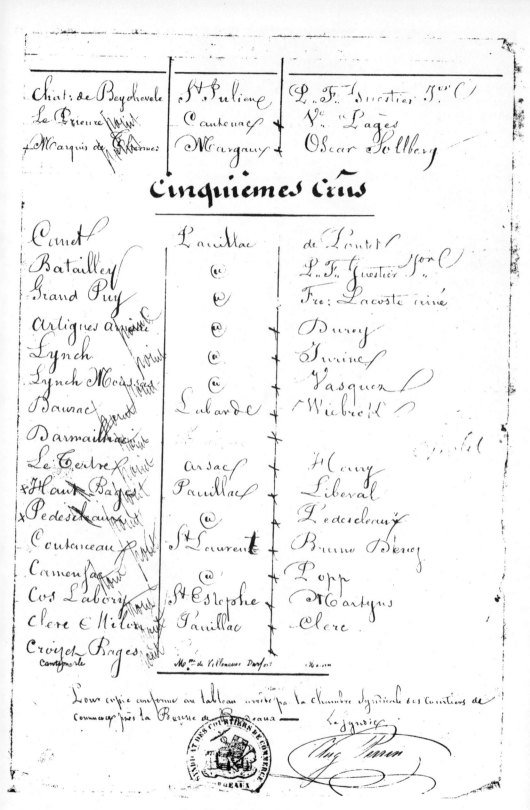

1855 Classification: Fifth Growth

PLATE III

Baron James Mayer de
Rothschild, who bought Château
Lafite in 1868.
Portrait by Delacroix

The Baroness Betty de
Rothschild, wife of Baron
James; the Second Empire
Rooms in the château
were her creation
Portrait by Ingres

PLATE IV

had been submitted, Margaux was ranked first by the brokers.[4] But Lafite had submitted only its 1846 and its 1848, still lacking bottle-age; Latour and Haut Brion had submitted no tasting samples, as such, at all, and it seems that tasting samples had been taken from the bottles on display.

The Chamber of Commerce had ruled, anyway at the beginning, that the classified wines should be ranked not according to this or to any other tasting, '*fait tout à fait accidental*', but according to the considered judgment of the *courtiers*. And thus Margaux's objection results in fact in a strengthening of Lafite's claim that the final order must be significant: it was the result of professional knowledge based on many years' experience, and not on an arbitrary and far from comprehensive single tasting of only a couple of recent vintages.

Conclusive support for the Lafite claim to be first among firsts was not long in coming, anyway. For whatever muddle there may have been in the minds of the Bordeaux Chamber of Commerce and the Syndicat des Courtiers in 1855 was miraculously cleared up by 1862, when a departmental commission of the Gironde, on which the Chamber of Commerce was represented, accepted an invitation to show the wines of the region at yet another Universal Exhibition, this time in London.

The official catalogue entry for the wines submitted, signed by the two delegates of the Jury Départemental de la Gironde,[5] stated specifically that the *crus classés*, which it listed precisely according to the 1855 classification, were ranked, within each category, according to merit: '*Les vins désignés sous le dénomination de* classes *sont divisés en cinq catégories et leur rang est indiqué selon leur mérite*'.

The same two delegates signed a pamphlet intended presumably for the Bordeaux Chamber of Commerce—it is among the Chamber's papers at the Bordeaux Municipal Library—*Note du*

---

[4] This must have been when the award of medals of honour was being considered: the classification, of course, had already been made.

[5] One of whom was T. B. G. Scott, no relation to the Scotts who then owned Lafite, but the British Consul at Bordeaux from 1832 to 1866 and a noted gourmet, famed even among the Bordelais for his knowledge of clarets, of which he had a remarkable collection.

Jury de la Gironde sur les Vins de Bordeaux envoyés à l'Exposition de Londres en 1862, which seems to make clear once and for all that the order must have been one of merit, for these are its comments on each of the first growths, listed in this order:

'*Le Château Lafite se distingue par son corps, une couleur et une sève supérieure à tout autre crû classé*';

Of Château Margaux: '*il est à observer que ce crû réussit moins souvent que Château Lafite, mais lorsqu'il arrive à parfait maturité, aucun vin ne peut le dépasser en qualité*';

Of Château Latour: '*digne emule de Château Lafite*';

And of Château Haut Brion: '*il manque à ce vin, pour atteindre la perfection des trois autres premiers crûs, le bouquet du Médoc, auquel il ne participe pas*'.

Nothing could seem clearer.

*　　　*　　　*

Emile Goudal, Scott's *gérant*, or director-general and agent, at Lafite (having taken over in 1834 from his father, who had been in charge since 1798) had behaved with abominable arrogance over the arrangements for the Exhibition and this, in a curious way, strengthens one's belief that his wine's claim to be first among the firsts must have been regarded as overwhelming. He irritated the Chamber of Commerce so much, and so often, that one is sure that if they could have thought of a good excuse for taking him and his wine down a peg, they would have jumped at it.

Against the express wish of the Chamber, clearly stated in a formal letter to Prince Napoleon, Goudal had succeeded not only in having his bottles of Lafite displayed separately from the other wines of the Médoc, but in having his own name and that of the proprietor put on the labels. (He accused the Chamber, composed largely of shippers, of wishing to put difficulties in the way of those who wished to buy directly from the estate, and of trying to make sure that they would have to go to the shippers. When he heard of the Chamber's letter to Prince Napoleon he stormed up to Paris, demanded a personal interview with the Prince, and got it. Napoleon took his side.)

The Chamber threatened Goudal that if, as a result of the

separate display, Château Lafite was awarded a special medal, they would insist that Château Margaux be put at the top of an amended list of first growths, 'lest all the honours should fall upon' Lafite.

In the event, all the first growths received medals (which incensed Goudal), and there was no change in the order.

* * *

There are now, and there must have been in 1855, nearly four hundred named growths in the Haut-Médoc alone—not including what was then known as the Bas-Médoc, or any of the other great regions, such as St Emilion, Pomerol, and the Graves, that lie around Bordeaux. In the whole region of the Bordelais there may well be a couple of thousand named growths.

What the classification of 1855 did was to select from these a mere sixty-two peers of the realm, as it were—and I use the analogy deliberately, for there are five ranks of *crus classés*, as there are of the British peerage: Lafite, Château Margaux, Latour and Haut Brion are dukes; Mouton is the senior marquis; and if Palmer is an earl, then Beychevelle is a viscount, Cantemerle a baron.

After these come the *crus exceptionnels*, the *crus bourgeois*, and the *crus artisans*, as we might refer to baronets, knights and esquires.

But let us not pursue the analogy too far. What is important is to realize that any claret listed in the 1855 classification is entitled to regard itself as a nobleman, being one of a mere sixty-odd chosen from a couple of thousand to appear in the Debrett of clarets.

This is much more to the point than to think of a fifth growth as being in some sense *fifth rate* as compared with a first. And just as it is the custom in England to refer to every peer other than a duke simply as 'Lord', whether he is a marquis or a baron, so each of the classified clarets refers to itself on its label not as a second or a third, a fourth or a fifth, but as a *grand cru classé du Médoc*—a lord.

Just as in any noble family the particular holder of the title at any given time may be a more agreeable, or a better-looking, or a more intelligent person than his father or his grandfather, so in any one year a particular classed growth may be better than recent years of the same wine.

More confusing still, the lesser growth's wine of a good year may be better than a finer growth in an 'off' year.

This is why, to give as permanent a validity as they could to their classification, the brokers of 1855 took into account not only the prices commanded by each wine for some time past[6] but also the soil and sub-soil of each vineyard, and the way its slopes took the sun, and drained themselves.

How sound their judgment was in general has been confirmed by Mr Ronald Barton, who wrote in 1963,[7] after forty years of first-hand experience at his own vineyards:

'Basically the classification remains sound, for it is based on the soil and the sub-soil and this has not changed. Given equal conditions a second can still, and will normally, produce a better wine than a third, a third than a fourth, and so on . . . The perfect proof of this is to be found in the vineyards of Léoville-Barton and Langoa. The two vineyards are run as one property and equal care is bestowed on both. And yet it can be said that always, whether the wine be good, bad or indifferent, the Léoville turns out to be the superior of the two.'

(Léoville was classified in 1855 as a second growth, Langoa as a third.)

All the same, changes do happen. Again to quote Mr Barton, 'some wines lost their popularity through lack of attention to the vines and to vinification while others increased in popularity through improved methods of cultivation, their ability to produce a wine more to the taste of the public, or again through increased publicity'. Estates are bought and sold, or split up, or merged.

For some time past, in consequence, there has been a movement among certain claret-growers of the Médoc either to have the 1855 classification modified or, leaving that untouched as a sort of museum piece, to have an entirely new one drawn up.

---

[6] According to the brokers' covering letter to their classification, first growths at the time fetched 3,000 *francs* a *tonneau*; seconds, 2,500 to 2,700; thirds, 2,100 to 2,400; fourths, 1,800 to 2,100; and fifths, 1,400 to 1,600.

[7] In his article, 'How the Clarets were Classified', in *The Compleat Imbiber*, No. 6.

M. Alexis Lichine, of Châteaux Lascombes and Prieuré, author of *The Wines of France,* has been a leading spirit among the would-be reformers, and has widely circulated his proposed new classification, most recently in the *Encyclopaedia of Wines and Spirits,* published in New York in 1967, but not published, I understand, in France.

M. Lichine also records in his encyclopaedia that in 1960 the Institut National des Appellations d'Origine was asked to consider the problem, but was judged by the interested bodies in Bordeaux, a couple of years later, to be too limited in its jurisdiction, since when the proposed reforms have been under discussion—not, it would appear, very urgent discussion—by the Bordeaux Chambre de Commerce and the Académie des Vins de Bordeaux. All I believe that has been achieved so far is that it has been made mandatory, when the 1855 classification is reproduced in whole or in part, or quoted, to specify that it *is* that of 1855.

I have had it confirmed by others that these discussions are taking place. Meanwhile, M. Lichine weakens both his own case for reform and the authority of his encyclopaedia by printing therein, as indeed he did in his *Wines of France,* not only his proposed revision, but also what he describes without qualification as, 'The Official Classification of the Great Growths of the Gironde: Classification of 1855', but in which he has promoted, without comment, his own Château Lascombes from ninth place in the list of second growths to second, immediately after Mouton, and his own Château Prieuré to the top of the fourth growths from being next to the bottom. He has made other changes, too, equally unforgivable and even less understandable. Whatever this list is, it is not the 1855 classification, and whatever the principles upon which M. Lichine works, they are not those of an encyclopaedist.

What is significant, in a study of Lafite, is that in M. Lichine's proposed new classification, as in every other unofficial essay I have seen on the same subject, Lafite remains where it was in 1855, at the top of the first growths. M. Lichine goes so far as to state that the wines in his top class—*Crus Hors Classe*—which is exactly that of the 1855 first growths (but with Mouton added as the fifth of them, promoted from the top of the seconds, followed by Châteaux Cheval Blanc, Ausone and Petrus, from St Emilion and Pomerol), are *not* in alphabetical order.

In other words, he is specific where some, at any rate, claim to find the 1855 classification equivocal: he places Lafite first among the firsts.

This explains why everyone at Lafite affects an air of lofty indifference whenever the question of reclassification comes up. Lafite was first among firsts in 1855: it would be first among firsts now, is their attitude: why should we concern ourselves?

But the fact that, of all the Médoc wines, Mouton is the only one that would be moved up, by common consent, from the second growths to the first (whatever title each category is given) also explains why it is that Baron Philippe de Rothschild, of Château Mouton-Rothschild, is in the forefront of the would-be reformers.

The dignified disdain of the motto adopted by his grandfather after the 1855 classification, (based on Rohan's '*Roi ne peux, Prince ne veux . . .*'):[8]

> '*Premier ne puis,*
> *Second ne daigne,*
> *Mouton suis*'

is belied by the vociferous indignation of the present owner. No use saying—to fall back on my earlier analogy—that few of us commoners feel that there is much difference between the premier marquis and a duke; or to add that if it is high price and great prestige that concern him, Mouton has both.

Nor is it of use to point out to Baron Philippe, as I have heard it pointed out over his dinner-table, that the Coldstream are the second regiment of Foot Guards; that their motto, not unlike that of Mouton, is *Nulli Secundus*, and that they live up to it without making a to-do, though their position in the line and the placing of their buttons remind them every day that officially they are second to the Grenadiers: neither the regiment itself nor anyone else considers it to be less soldierly, or in any way inferior.

---

[8] Another version is: '*Roi ne puis,*
          Prince ne daigne,
          Rohan suis.'

No, he argues: his wine fetches the same price as a first growth, and has done for these past thirty years or so, sometimes level-pegging with Lafite;[9] it is a gross injustice to the wine, and misleading to the public, to go on calling Mouton a second growth.

Baron Philippe is a man of immense charm, talent and energy. Unlike most other Rothschilds, he has no bank to bother with, and so can devote his time to his wine, his collections, and his translations from the English—at one time, the plays of Christopher Fry; now, largely from the Elizabethan poets.

With his similarly charming, talented and energetic American wife, he keeps open house at Château Mouton on a princely scale, dispensing the most exquisite food, accompanied by Mouton of the finest and rarest vintages, to monarchs and millionaires; poets and painters; dons and dilettante; and, above all, to amateurs of and writers about wine.

Thus, his strongly held and vehemently expressed opinions about the classification of 1855 are canvassed by those particularly interested, unusually articulate, and especially influential—much more so than any views on this particular subject expressed, if he expresses any at all, by his cousin Baron Elie, who is virtually never in residence at Lafite, though he is fully in control of it; has other things besides wine to think about, as have most of his closest friends; and is perfectly content with Lafite's unquestioned position at the top of a century-old tree.

Naturally enough, in so much talk about Mouton's grievances, some of it well-informed, some of it mere gossip, the tendency is to regard the whole matter as one of Rothschild *versus* Rothschild: an endless, unedifying family squabble between cousins— one, it is hinted, arrogant; the other, it is suggested, envious.

This is to do both Baron Philippe and Baron Elie a good deal less than justice. It may well be—it could hardly be otherwise— that the fact that they *are* cousins has given a sharpness to the rivalry: it has certainly given it a piquancy for outsiders.

The fact of the matter, though, is that the rivalry between the two châteaux dates from a time before there was a Rothschild at either. The feeling between Mouton and Lafite is a feeling as between two great wines, very different in style but very similar in

9 See Appendix II, p. 138.

prestige, made next door to each other and fetching similar prices, of which one was classed as a first growth long before the classification of 1855, which simply confirmed its standing, the other as a second.

It is a sort of Oxford and Cambridge, Sotheby's and Christie's rivalry, but as if intensified by one of these two universities, one of these two salerooms, having been officially ranked, in 1855 or earlier, as slightly the inferior of the two. It would be the same if there were a Mr Jones at Mouton and a Mr Smith at Lafite—this happened when there was, in fact, a Baron Brane at the one, a Samuel Scott at the other: when there was not a Rothschild at either.

Cocks, in 1846, was writing of Mouton as 'an excellent second growth'; in 1847, Biarnez—'the enthusiastic bard of the Bacchus of Bordeaux', as Warner Allen called him—was writing, in his limp alexandrines:

> *Qui croirait que Mouton, modeste autant que grand,*
> *Ne vient qu'après Laffitte et n'est qu'au second rang?*
> *Cependant le gourmet ne peut le méconnaître:*
> *Il a même valeur, plus de valeur peut-être,*
> *Et chacun, ébahi, se demande pourquoi*
> *Mouton, le grand Mouton, n'a pas le nom de roi.*

Not only was Mouton already feeling wounded, so long ago as that, about its being in the second rank: it was specifically Lafite's position in the first—not Latour's, not Margaux's—that was the salt in the wound.

This was not only before the classification of 1855: it was before Baron Nathaniel de Rothschild had bought Mouton, in May 1853. The owner of Mouton in the 1840s was a M. Thuret, who had bought it from the great wine-grower, Baron Brane, or Branne, in 1830, had never done particularly well with it (in spite of that, *'il a même valeur, plus de valeur peut-être'*), and who took a loss of some 75,000 francs when he sold to Baron Nathaniel.

Nathaniel was a younger son, born in 1812, of Nathan Mayer Rothschild, that one of the five brothers from Frankfurt who had settled in London, and founded the English family.[10] He had decided, after becoming partially paralysed by a fall in the hunting-

[10] See Chapter 4.

field, to settle in Paris where, according to Mr Frederic Morton, he 'collected masterpieces', and 'kept a brilliant salon'—very much, indeed, as his great-grandson, Baron Philippe, does at Mouton to this day.

Thus, Baron Nathaniel was an Englishman by birth and a banker, though no longer an active one, by family connection. Emil Goudal, the manager of Lafite, was at once on his toes to protect the prestige and the interest of his own English banker: Mr Samuel Scott, his employer.[11]

At more than one point the Lafite and the Mouton properties not only march with, but actually dovetail into each other. The most important point was, and still is, at the western edge of the Mouton property, where some fifty acres of Lafite's Carruades vineyards jut eastwards between Mouton's.

Very slight eminences, the Carruades have always grown fine wine, either because of the way the slopes catch the sun, or because the sub-soil drains well. When Baron Nathaniel bought Mouton, these Carruades vineyards were only recent additions to Lafite: it is clear from a letter of September 26, 1852, that Goudal had bought them for the elder Scott at some time between 1830 and 1849, and had only just prevented their falling into the hands of the then owner of Mouton, M. Thuret.

For some reason, in the early 1850s, just before and just after Nathaniel Rothschild bought Mouton, the younger Scott was of a mind to sell them again, and Goudal's anxiety lest Mouton should get hold of them—whether M. Thuret's Mouton, before May 1853, or Baron Nathaniel's Mouton, after that date—shows how determined he was to hold on to every advantage he had against his next-door neighbour. Latour and Château Margaux were also first growths of the Médoc—Latour also a near neighbour in Pauillac—but it was Mouton that was always regarded as Lafite's nearest rival, and not only geographically.

[11] Sir Samuel Scott, 2nd Bt., had died in 1849, to be succeeded in the baronetcy by his elder son, Claude; but as putative owner of Lafite, or as its controller at the family bank (the curious question of precise ownership at this time is discussed in Chapter 4) by a younger son, also called Samuel— born 1807, died 1869. It is to this Samuel Scott that the letters I quote from later in this chapter are addressed.

'During a good year', Goudal wrote to Samuel Scott, 'the
Carruades can give a big profit'; adding how nearly Mouton had
bought these vineyards in the time of Scott's father. On November 6, 1852, when it was still M. Thuret, not Baron Nathaniel,
at Mouton, Goudal writes: '. . . it is difficult to give a value to the
Carruades . . . [they] are worth 200,000 francs to Mouton, and
are not worth 100,000 to a small landlord. Our lawyer is very
surprised at this question, and considers that anyone advising
you to sell the Carruades is your enemy, these vineyards being
the best in Pauillac . . .' 'The Carruades were bought by your
father, and planted with the intention of mixing their wine with
that of the older vineyards.'

And again, a week later, such was Goudal's perturbation: 'I
must tell you that there is not a vineyard in your old property as
valuable as the Carruades . . . they can only increase the value of
your wine.' And in January 1853: 'Again, I consider the Carruades as the best land in the Médoc.'

By the end of May of that year there was a new owner at
Mouton, and in August Goudal is on the defensive: 'If you still
want to sell the Carruades, I could talk to the manager of Mouton,
and see if M. Rothschild is interested. But I persist in saying that
the Carruades are your best land . . .'

In a matter of weeks, though, he is on the attack, and writes,
on September 27: 'Since my last letter of August 28 about the
Carruades, I took advice from friends on the consequences that
the sale of this land would have. They were unanimous. The sale
of the Carruades to M. Rothschild would be very improper and
could have for you the most disastrous consequences. *This is very
serious*. If M. Rothschild would buy the Carruades, which are
appreciated by everybody as vineyards of the highest quality,
which can do good to any wine it will be mixed with, M. Rothschild having great wealth will try to get Mouton made a first
growth. Do you realize the consequence this will have for you?
Mouton as a first growth could only depreciate Lafite. While if
you are selling the Carruades to another person, you will not have
this problem. I told you once that the Mouton owner was the
only one able to give you a good price for your Carruades. But
at this time I did not know yet how good its wines were and how

much they could improve the Mouton wines. Therefore, it would be better to sell the Carruades for 50,000 francs to a stranger than for 50,000 more than that to M. Rothschild. I tell you all this so that you can think about it. As for the price to ask anybody else, I would say 200,000 francs, although I doubt we can get this price for the Carruades, as it has no house.'

Eventually, in October 1853, a broadside: 'I would repeat, sir, what I have had the honour of telling you many times; that is, that if I had ever thought that one day you would sell this property [the Carruades] I would never have talked the late Sir Samuel into this business [of buying it]. Be persuaded, sir, that you own one of the finest properties in the Médoc: that is the general opinion.'

Like many a resident manager for an absentee landlord, Emil Goudal had his way, and from then on we hear no more of selling the Carruades, which have always remained Lafite property. (They still give their name to Lafite's second wine—Carruades de Château Lafite, which is made from those vines that are less than twelve years old, though these are no longer necessarily the vines of the Carruades vineyards: in time those have become senior, and Carruades de Château Lafite comes from whatever part of Lafite has, at a given time, the youngest vines.)

It is quite clear that it was the relative prestige of Mouton that Goudal was chiefly concerned about, and once there was no more danger of the Carruades' falling into its hands, he begins to fret about comparative prices. Again, it is Mouton, and not the first growths, that is in the forefront of his mind, and that we find mentioned by far the most frequently in his letters.

Once Baron Nathaniel is the owner, Goudal suspects Mouton of being up to all sorts of City banker's tricks: he writes in October 1856 of M. Johnston, the Bordeaux merchant, that he is, 'associated in business with Baron Rothschild, and to please that banker (and certainly to his own advantage), helps him in his aim to place his wine on a level with the firsts'. The insinuation was that Johnston bought Mouton at a higher price than it was worth for the sake of some under-the-counter deal or other advantage, and thus gave Mouton a prestige that it did not deserve.

The ancient rivalry was felt all the more keenly now that there was a Rothschild at Mouton, however far it must have been from Emile Goudal's mind that there would ever be a Rothschild at Lafite. He wrote gloatingly to Scott of 'the revenge we took on Baron Rothschild', when he refused to sell the 1856 Lafite until he had found out what Mouton was being offered at, and reached in consequence a record price of 5,700 francs: 'he (Baron Nathaniel) prided himself a little too soon on having sold at the same price as Lafite, even for the 1855 . . . our revenge was not long in coming . . . Rely on me to uphold the honour of the flag'.

Similar sentiments have been expressed often enough, one feels sure, in the century or so since then, and at both châteaux. But it is very clear that 'the honour of the flag' had been felt to be at stake before there was a Rothschild at either—before, indeed, the classification of 1855 which, by fixing right up to our own time the distinction between first growth and second, made the traditional rivalry all the more intense.[12]

In any case, family rivalry is one thing, family solidarity another, and the two are not incompatible. When Philippine, the actress daughter of Baron Philippe de Rothschild of Mouton, was married at Pauillac on March 4, 1961, to M. Jacques Sereys, of the Comédie Française, guests were put up at Lafite as well as at Mouton, and when all the guests were gathered together at the three great meals that were served, two at Mouton and one at Lafite, subtle courtesies were exchanged in each château's choice of wines.

Thus, at dinner at Mouton on the evening before the wedding, the 1895 Lafite was served between the 1921 and the 1870 Mouton, but at luncheon there next day—the wedding day—Mouton magnanimously gave pride of place to the 1869 Lafite, with

[12] Baron Philippe ought at any rate to feel flattered that locally 'Rothschild' always means Mouton, never Lafite. A man will say that he is going to work for the Rothschilds, and it will be understood that he is going to Mouton. A letter addressed to the Rothschilds will be delivered to Mouton and, indeed, there is a big modern mural painting in the post office at Pauillac, depicting a panoramic view of the commune's *vignoble*: Mouton is marked simply as 'Château Rothschild', Lafite as 'Château Lafite'.

precedence over (which in this case, of course, means that it came *after*) both the 1933 and the 1928 Mouton.

In a handsome return gesture that evening, at dinner in the *chai* at Lafite, that château's own 1949 and 1926 served to lead up to the 1869 Mouton.[13]

Who would not wish to have tasted those two 1869 clarets on that one spring day in 1961?

M. André Simon has recalled, in his *The Noble Grapes and Great Wines of France*, drinking a bottle of what he calls the 'astounding' 1869 Lafite in 1954: 'it was incredibly good! Not merely alive, but lively; ruby red, not pink; fairly sweet still; very smooth, gentle and charming, its bouquet discreet but intensely clean'. While H. Warner Allen, in his *Natural Red Wines*, wrote of the 'tremendous Mouton 1869, a paragon of velvety silkiness and hidden depths of significant magnificence', and classed it as the finest 1869 claret he had ever tasted. He did not state in what year that was, but his book was published in 1951.

If both these wines were drinking as well in 1961—and as M. Simon found no sign of its approaching end in the Lafite in 1954, and as they had both come from the cellars of their respective châteaux, and been handled and served with meticulous care, I have no doubt that they were—these must indeed have been memorable meals.

There is something majestic in a rivalry that has wines of this sort being matched against each other.

[13] The other wines served at the three meals were the 1949 and the 1953 Mouton Baron Philippe (which used to be called Mouton d'Armailhacq), the 1947 Pol Roger, the 1934 and the famous 1921 Yquem as dessert wines, and the same château's 1945 in the middle of dinner with *pâté de foie gras*, as is the custom in the Bordelais.

4. The Rothschild Purchase

THE vane on the top of the pepper-pot clock-tower at Château Lafite is formed of five arrows, joined in the middle, so that heads and feathers all fan outwards.

This is a Rothschild symbol, common to all branches of the family: an 'arm embowed proper' grasps five arrows in the third and in the fourth quarters of the arms of Lord Rothschild, head of the English branch. (The same device provides an inn-sign at Waddesdon and possibly in other Chiltern villages that once depended on a Rothschild at the big house.)

The five arrows symbolize the five brothers who, during Napoleon's time, set out from their father's house in the Frankfurt ghetto to conquer Europe. Their victories were more lasting than those of their great contemporary.

The eldest, Amschel, though he left the ghetto, remained in his native city to head the family bank and to become eventually treasurer of Bismarck's infant German Confederation.

Salomon became rich and powerful in Vienna; Kalmann (Carl) in Naples.

Nathan went to England to become probably the richest and

most powerful of them all, and the youngest, Jacob (James), went to Paris in 1811, at the age of nineteen, speaking no French.

There is no doubt that James began his social career in Paris as something of a thruster. Captain Gronow, recalling in his debt-ridden old age[1] the days when he was a twenty-two-year-old officer of Foot Guards in the Allied forces occupying Paris, tells of a ball at the British Embassy in 1816:

'During the reign of the Bourbons, society was, as now, divided into two or more classes; the nobility on the one hand, and the rich mercantile men on the other. The latter studiously copied their betters in dress, manner, and style of living; but as a system of exclusiveness was observed, which militated against their being admitted into the best *salons*, great interest was necessary to overcome the obstacle to their admission. A beautiful woman, the wife of a rich banker, being desirous of getting an invitation to a *bal costumé* given at the British Embassy in Paris, induced Mr James Rothschild, the great financier, to ask Lady Elizabeth Stuart, the Ambassadress, for an invitation. The *entrée* being obtained by means of a ticket obtained by stealth from Sir Charles Stuart, the lady set about choosing a costume, and decided on appearing as Diana; but not having been classically educated, she did not bear in mind that chastity was a distinguishing characteristic of the goddess she intended to represent. The consequence was, that her apperance was such as to lead any one, not versed in Greek mythology, to suppose that the country in which Diana hunted must have lain in some happy region near the equator, where the scantiest drapery was the most agreeable costume. The lady, with a triumphant air, that was regarded as effrontery, entered the ballroom dressed, or rather undressed, as described, and approached the British Ambassadress, who, astonished at the exhibition, turned her back, and studiously avoided compromising herself by even looking at the lady during the rest of the evening; informing the visitors present, her friends, that the "Jew" was alone responsible for the immodest appearance of this representative of the chaste goddess.'

The 'great financier' was then twenty-four.

By 1821—just thirty, and still with the strong German accent

[1] *Captain Gronow's Last Recollections*, 1865.

that he never lost—James was consul-general for the Austrian Empire in Paris and a baron, and had bought the great Palais Fouché in the Rue Laffitte that had once belonged to Napoleon's chief of police.

Success, wealth, and his family connections, already legendary, helped to establish James in Paris society, but what consolidated his position was his marriage, in 1824, to his niece, Betty, daughter of his elder brother Salomon, when he was thirty-two and she was just nineteen, and everything that her uncle-husband was not: a beauty, a charmer, and socially adroit.

As it was the British Ambassadress who, in Gronow's story, snubbed James's *protegée* at the Embassy, it is fitting that it should be another British Ambassadress, Lady Granville, whose husband had been appointed to Paris in the year that James and Betty married, who wrote to her sister, Lady Carlisle:

'On Saturday we dined at a sumptuous feast at Rothschild's. He has married his niece, a pretty little Jewess, *née coiffée*,[2] a very good thing at Paris, for just out of her nursery she does the honours of her house as if she had never done anything else.'

Now the Rothschild palace in the Rue Laffitte (still part of the Rothschild bank buildings) came to life: James had Carême to cook his meals there; Heine to sing his praises; Rossini to compose music for his parties; and Balzac to dedicate stories both to Baron James and to Baroness Betty—and to borrow their money.

Delacroix painted James's portrait (Plate IVa), and Ingres, after declining for two years repeated commissions to paint Betty's, then saw the lady, changed his mind, and spent another five years over the task (Plate IVb). The painting was one of the most eye-catching at the great Ingres centenary Exhibition at the Petit Palais in the winter of 1967–1968: 'sumptuous', wrote the correspondent of the *New Yorker*—'. . . at ease in silks, with a double elegance inherited from both sides of her privileged family, and in her relaxation as graceful as a hothouse rose beginning to shed its petals.' It was all the more an attraction at the Exhibition as having rarely before been seen in public, for it had never been out of the family's possession since it left the studio: it belongs now to Baron Guy de Rothschild, the sitter's eldest

[2] 'Born with a silver spoon in her mouth.'

Catherine Serebriakoff 1961

The Château and the *Chais*
Painting by Catherine Serebriakoff

PLATE V

Front of Château from the terrace garden, showing the Rothschild five
arrows above the pepper-pot tower
Painting by Catherine Serebriakoff

PLATE VI

great-grandson, by whose permission it is reproduced in this book.

It was James who bought Château Lafite, but that was in his old age, in 1868, when he had outlived not only his four brothers, but as many French régimes—those of Napoleon, Louis XVIII, Charles X and Louis-Philippe. Less than a couple more years, and he would have outlived a fifth.

In less than half a century, 'fox-faced and sandy-haired' James, with his guttural accent,—'a happy mixture of the French dandy and the orange boy',[3] (for his clothes were more elegant than his manners) had created the French railways; had survived a gigantic fraud that cost his bank its entire cash assets of six million francs; and had emerged the victor from a great financial struggle against two other French-Jewish families of bankers, those of Achille Fould and Emile Pereire.

By the eighteen-sixties, James, now a baron of the French as well as of the Austrian empire, was not only the richest man in France but the most powerful and the least vulnerable.

So much so, that as the Baroness Betty was so ardent an Orléanist that she would not make the curtsey to Napoleon III, the Emperor invited himself to the Rothschilds' vast palace of Ferrières, outside Paris, saying as he gave her his arm to dinner: 'Madame, you would not visit me; so, as I much wished to make your acquaintance, *I* am obliged to be *your* guest.'

In the summer of 1868, Baron James was seventy-six years old, and a sick man. He was suffering, like his Emperor, from gall-stones, and now he had fallen victim to jaundice.

Why did this aged invalid take on the purchase of Château Lafite? Although it went for a record sum, it was small beer—if that is the appropriate word—to the great financier, and we have no evidence that he was especially fond of its wine or, indeed, of claret in general. The only story linking him with the wine of Lafite before he bought the château is the one that finds him at the table of Baron Haussmann pouring his Lafite from one glass into another, and adding water, saying:

'*Puisque tu m' as trompé; je vais le tremper à mon tour!*'—'As you've deceived (trompé) me, I shall dilute *you*!' Whether this was a

[3] Cecil Roth, *The Magnificent Rothschilds*, London 1939.

criticism of Lafite, or of Haussmann's choice of it, is difficult to say.

And the only other story that brings together the baron and the bottle concerns a dinner party *en famille* to which Heine had been invited.

That evening, the poet was morose, and Baron James sought to loosen his tongue by plying him with his finest wines, eventually working up—so the story goes, and one cannot imagine what the preceding, inferior wines must have been—to a bottle of Lacrima Christi.

Heine still sat mumchance, and Baron James rallied him: this was the noblest Lacrima Christi, and he still had not a word to say about this splendid wine!

At last, Heine broke his silence.

'Do you know,' he asked, 'why it is called Lacrima Christi?'
'Why?'

'These are Christ's tears,' Heine said, 'because he weeps at the sight of two wicked Jews like us drinking such a precious wine when there are thousands of poor Christians in Paris without a crust of bread.'

Others might have wept at the thought that Lacrima Christi was one of the finest wines in the cellar of the man who was eventually to buy Lafite.

This story, of course, is *ben trovato*—I take it from Ignatius Balla's gossipy *Romance of the Rothschilds*—but it makes a relevant point about Baron James's taste, and encourages one to accept the opinion of Baron Elie, James's great-grandson, now part owner and present effective controller of Lafite, that the old man was pushed into the purchase by his sons. Baron Elie told me that he has seen somewhere among the family papers a letter in which James urges the young men to remember that 'we are bankers: we are not agriculturists', or words very much to that effect.

There is no evidence that James ever set foot on the property, either before or after he bought it.[4] Indeed, there would have

[4] The suggestion that Baron James bought Château Lafite in a fit of whimsy because he had lived, and still conducted his business, in Rue Laffitte, shows little understanding of the Rothschilds in general and of this Rothschild in particular: James was not given to whimsy, nor was he at this time in a fit state for it.

been little time after the purchase: it was bought on August 8, 1868 and James died little more than three months later, on November 15—the day after his friend, Rossini.

James's sons were Alphonse, then forty-one; Gustave, thirty-nine; and Edmond, a mere twenty-three. (Another son, Salomon, had died before the Lafite purchase.)

Their interest in Lafite is understandable. All three of them entertained on a princely—nay, an imperial—scale. They collected: paintings and jewels; books and bibelots; great palaces and great heiresses—for just as their father had married his niece, and one of their sisters an English Rothschild cousin (Nathan's son), so Alphonse, too, married a Rothschild cousin from England (Nathan's daughter), and Edmond one from Frankfurt, which made them all richer than ever.

As collectors, then, why not collect the greatest of all French vineyards? As hosts, they would have the pleasure not only of serving the finest claret but of knowing—and knowing that their guests knew—that it was their own. And they were rich enough to be able to indulge their wish, and to do so as a private family deal, not as an enterprise of the bank's. Château Lafite is a private family property to this day.

Many factors, moreover, combined to make the prospective ownership of Lafite attractive at this particular time. It was not much more than a dozen years since the classification of 1855 had set an official seal on Lafite's pre-eminence among clarets: first of the first growths. There had been good vintages of Lafite since then: the 1861 Lafite was already famous (for the French then, as they do now, drank their clarets younger than the English do), and Alfred Danflou's book, published only the year before the purchase in Bordeaux, had proclaimed the 1864 and 1865 vintages of Lafite as both 'splendid and profitable', going on to observe that Lafite 'is nectar reserved for the gods of this world—that is to say, for those who are rich enough to pay for it'.

The 1864 proved, indeed, to be the most splendid and the most famous of all. Maurice Healy and Walter Berry sang its praises into the twenties and thirties of this century; to Warner Allen, who drank it first in 1904 and last in 1933, it was 'the most glorious wine I ever tasted'; and M. André Simon has recorded that it 'was quite outstanding for fully half a century, and it out-lived all the other great wines of that great vintage. As late as the early thirties, when it was very nearly seventy years old, the Lafite 1864 was wonderful; it was still fresh, soft and sweet, and its exquisite bouquet made me pause and wonder whether there is any age limit to a really great claret.'

In 1967 a magnum of this peerless wine was sold at Christie's for £82.

Nobody, of course, could have known in 1868 that the 1864 Lafite would have so long and so glorious a future, but it would have been realized already, as we knew in 1967 of the 1964s, that it was a great wine, with remarkable potentialities,—all the more so because, in those pre-phylloxera days, although good clarets were drunk young, yet the survivors were expected to be long-lived.

It seems unlikely that Alphonse, Gustave and Edmond, with the possible purchase of a *grand cru* of Bordeaux on their minds, would not have come across Alfred Danflou's book, which was called *Les Grands Crus Bordelais*, or would not have had it brought to their attention. In any case, they and their advisers and agents would have been well enough aware of the continuing prestige of Lafite, and that, in Danflou's words, they were 'rich enough to pay for it'—for the vines as well as for the wines.

Their English cousins were becoming masters of foxhounds, not to mention staghounds, and if the talented creator of John Jorrocks had recently made unkind game of this new race of Jewish sporting gentlemen in his portrait, in *Ask Mamma*, of Sir Moses Mainchance, Bt., M.F.H., that was all the more reason, perhaps, why French-Jewish gentlemen should buy vineyards, rather than set up as foxhunting men.

It was, indeed, as a result of a fall in the hunting field that their English cousin, Nathaniel (who was also their brother-in-law), was now the owner of Château Mouton, next door to Lafite. The fall had crippled him, making it impossible for him ever to ride again, and he elected to live in France rather than in England, and all the readier to do so, presumably, because of his marriage to Baron James's daughter, Charlotte. He bought Château Mouton—Brane-Mouton, as it was then—in 1853.

Two years later, at the Paris Exhibition, Mouton had been confirmed in its place as first of the second growths of the Gironde. Now that Lafite, first of the first growths, was on the market, it was an obvious temptation to his cousins and brothers-in-law to outdo him.

All the more so as, in the same year that Nathaniel bought Mouton, another Jewish banker had bought Château Palmer, classed as a third growth—their, and their father's, old rival, Emil Pereire.

The first two or three decades of the century had been hard times for the Médoc, so that the old families of wine-growing landlords were unable, when the oïdium struck, in the fifties, to stand the expense of poor crops in succession, chemical treatment, and waiting for better times.

A very large number of great vineyards changed hands, and the Paris financiers moved in. (And went on doing so after the 1855 classification. Only two proprietors' names are the same now as they were then—oddly enough, neither of them French: Barton at Langoa and Rothschild at Mouton. Barton had bought Langoa in the eighteen-twenties—he was a Bordeaux merchant, not a banker, but his purchase was part of the same trend.) The Aguados, Franco-Spanish bankers, and a family very close to that of the Empress, the Montijos, were the first: they bought Château Margaux in 1836. The Foulds, business rivals—like the Pereires—of the Rothschilds, were soon to be at Beychevelle, the Dollfuss family at Montrose. What packs of foxhounds were to financiers in London, so were the great claret vineyards to their opposite numbers in Paris.

*   *   *

Fiction is stranger than fact.

Those fictions are, at any rate, that have accumulated around the 1868 sale at which Baron James de Rothschild bought Lafite, and about its immediately previous ownership.

In the middle eighteenth century Lafite had belonged to the noble family of Ségur, owners also of Latour, Mouton and Calon, which bears the family name to this day. It was under the Ségur ownership that Lafite became famous, and the Comte de Ségur of the day nicknamed at Court *le prince des vignes*.

By the time of the Revolution, this vast property, or con-glomeration of properties, had already been split up, and Lafite —not the others—belonged to another aristocrat, Nicolas Pierre de Pichard, holder of various baronies in the Pauillac region, a member of the King's council, and president of the provincial *Parlement* of Guyenne at Bordeaux. His daughter, Anne-Marguerite-Marie-Adelaïde, was married to a Comte de Puységur, and there may well have been family connections between Pich-ard and Ségur, either through the Puységur alliance, or by blood.

Had Lafite, before the Revolution, remained in the hands of the Ségur family the later history of its ownership might well have been very different, for all the members of the family sur-vived the Revolution. One, indeed, who had been a marshal of France under the monarchy (and possibly the owner of Lafite), lived to receive a pension from Napoleon, under whom both his grandsons served, the one as a senator and grand master of cere-monies, the other as a general. It is to be supposed that they pre-served their properties intact.

But Anne-Marguerite-Marie-Adelaïde de Puységur and her husband fled the Revolution; they were proscribed as *emigrés*, and her parents arraigned as their accomplices, tried, and guillotined. As an *emigrée*, the daughter had forfeited her right to inherit, and Lafite became the property of the French Republic, on behalf of which it was put up for auction, on Fructidor 15, year V of the republic—September 2, 1797.[5]

It is at this point that the story becomes complicated. I shall attempt drastically to simplify, where some have romanticized without clarifying.

Lafite was bought in 1797 by a Dutch syndicate. In various French official documents the owners are named variously: some-times Lafite is described as belonging to the M. de Witt who acted for the syndicate, sometimes as belonging equally to its

[5] In 1825, the Comte de Puységur, to whom his wife, being childless, had conveyed her patrimony, applied for compensation out of funds set aside under the Restoration for those returned *emigrés* whose property had been sold by the Republic. He was awarded 2,185,000 francs—a very reasonable amount for a property that had been sold for 2,003,000, even allowing for changes in the meantime in the value of money.

three members, all Dutch, whose names need not concern us here, and who did not include de Witt.

In 1803, Lafite was bought from the syndicate for 1,200,000 francs by Ignace-Joseph Vanlerberghe,[6] grain merchant, financier, army contractor, and at about this time Napoleon's Head of General Supplies. Vanlerberghe was an associate of Gabriel Julien Ouvrard, a notorious speculator of the time, and the pair of them went into bankruptcy in 1808. (It is an odd coincidence that in 1830 Ouvrard was to be involved in a money battle with the Rothschilds, from which he emerged very much the loser.) Proceedings between Vanlerberghe and his principal creditors were still dragging on at the time of Vanlerberghe's death, in 1819, just before which, in 1818, he transferred Lafite to his wife, Barbe-Rosalie Lemaire, for the consideration of one million francs.

Undoubtedly, this was in order to keep the property out of the hands of Vanlerberghe's creditors, and this in spite of the fact that Vanlerberghe and Barbe-Rosalie Lemaire were divorced —and divorced twice over, in 1794 and in 1800.

Presumably Vanlerberghe had been in difficulties in 1800, for the second divorce had also been intended to keep Lafite in the family, by quashing, as the first divorce had failed to do, any agreement as to husband and wife's common ownership of the Vanlerberghe property, under which Lafite would have been forfeited to his creditors.

There were doubts about the effectiveness of this divorce (well-founded doubts, as it turned out, for in 1827 it was declared null), and in 1821 Barbe-Rosalie Lemaire sold Lafite for the same sum she had paid for it—one million francs—to Mr Samuel Scott.

Now Mr Samuel Scott (not M. Schott, as some French writers have had it, and not Sir Harry, as he has been styled by a number

[6] In various histories of Lafite, I have come across no fewer than five different spellings of the name, from Vandemère to Van den Berghe. The one I give here is that given in French legal documents of 1856 and 1868, and must be regarded as the one that finds official favour.

Under whatever spelling, he is always stated to have been a Dutchman—presumably because of his name and also the previous Dutch ownership of the property. In fact, although no doubt of Belgian or Flemish origin, he was born a Frenchman, in Douai, in 1758, and he was the father-in-law of Napoleon's General Rapp.

of English writers who should have known better, the one copying the other) was the only son of Sir Claude Scott, to whose baronetcy he succeeded in 1830. Samuel was a member of Parliament, and a senior partner in his father's eminently respectable London bank, Sir Claude Scott, Bart., and Co., of 1, Cavendish Square—a bank later to be known as Sir Samuel Scott, Bart., and Co., before being taken over in 1894 by Parr's Bank, and eventually merged into the Westminster.

So much for a figure that one distinguished English writer has styled, 'the enigmatic and apparently not too scrupulous Baronet', —a perfectly respectable banker, in fact, who bought Lafite, as the bank later testified, '*pour compte et avec les deniers de M. Aimé-Eugène Vanlerberghe*'—on the account of, and with the money of, that is, Ignace-Joseph Vanlerberghe's son, for whom strict accounts were kept at the Scott bank—one ledger still survives in the Westminster Bank's archives.

Here, then, is yet another myth exploded—the story, again copied from one writer by another, of the younger Vanlerberghe (but the name spelled wrong, of course) cheated of his inheritance, wandering morosely through the vineyards that should rightly have been his 'in the blazing sunshine of August'—such are the touches of verisimilitude—'doing his best to protect himself from its heat under the shade of a vast parasol of red silk. Eventually, after many years, he died of melancholy or apoplexy.'

Nonsense!

Vanlerberghe *fils* knew exactly what he was doing, and was far from being defrauded. When his father died, in 1819, he had accepted his inheritance, whereas his three sisters declined it. Two years later, with what must have been his full cognizance, Lafite was bought by a respectable London banking house with his money and on his behalf, but this fact was kept secret, lest it fall into the hands of his father's creditors. (It was not until 1856 that the Tribunal Civil de la Seine declared the Vanlerberghe inheritance free of any further claims.) The Lafite property was managed by the excellent—indeed a famous—*régisseur*, Emil Goudal, and its finances were administered by the bank, to which Goudal wrote regular detailed reports—first to Mr (later Sir Samuel) Scott, and then to his younger son, also Samuel.

It was not until the younger Vanlerberghe's death, in 1866, that the bank registered a formal declaration that it had bought and administered Lafite on his behalf. This in order that the property could be put up to *vente sur licitation*—an auction held to determine the value, or to make possible the division, of an otherwise indivisible property to which there is a number of heirs, in this case Vanlerberghe's three sisters and a niece.

This, then, is how Lafite came to be for sale in the summer of 1868, to the great excitement of the shippers and *négociants* of Bordeaux and the growers of the Médoc, not only because of the great prestige of the estate, the fame of its *régisseur*, and the potential of its vineyards, but also because it was well known that its recent vintages, still in cask, were immensely valuable and that the cellars of the château held the finest collection of old wines in the region.

That the Rothschilds were interested was known, or very strongly suspected, and a syndicate of Bordeaux merchants was formed to buy Lafite, headed by a M. de Guernon, anxious to prevent yet another noble Médoc estate—this time, indeed, the noblest,—from falling into the hands of another of those banking fellows from Paris, as Château Margaux and Château Mouton had done. (It may be that it was the Rothschild already at Mouton, not James's branch of the family, that was thought to be interested: it would have been a natural supposition.)

Yet, when Lafite was first put up for sale in Bordeaux, on July 20, 1868, the reserve price of four and a half million francs for the Lafite property, plus a quarter of a million for the Carruades (some £190,000 in all at that time) was not reached, and the property was withdrawn. With both the Rothschilds and the Bordeaux syndicate so keen, this seems odd, and all the odder in the light of what the Rothschilds' agent is said to have boasted after the subsequent sale—that he had ten million francs at his disposal. Bertall, in his *La Vigne*, which was published in 1878, when memories of the sale must still have been fairly fresh, stated that the syndicate commanded six million. I have been unable to find, in the newspaper reports or the gossip writers of the time, any explanation of the failure of this first sale, but in addition to the reserve price of four and a half million, there were taxes to be paid and the 1868 crop to be bid for separately: it may be that the syndicate's six million did not stretch so far, and that the Rothschilds' agent was not told that he had ten million to play with until it was seen that more, at any rate, than six million would be needed.

However that may be, the property was then put up in Paris, at the Palais de Justice, on August 8, 1868, with the reserve reduced to three million francs for the Lafite property: the reserve of a quarter of a million on the Carruades seems not to have been altered. The bidding was brisk and brief, and Lafite and Carruades were knocked down to agents acting on behalf of the Baron James de Rothschild for a total sum of 4,440,000 francs (some £177,000), made up of 4,140,000 francs for Lafite itself and 300,000 for the Carruades vineyards. There were fees and taxes in addition, to the tune of some 400,000 francs, or £16,000.

Château Margaux had been sold to the Aguados in 1836 for 1,300,000 francs; Château Mouton to cousin Nathaniel in 1853 for either 1,125,000 or 1,175,000 (the authorities differ: there may have been two lots, as with Lafite and the Carruades); Château Palmer to the rival banking family of Pereire in 1853 for a mere 425,000 (though the property was smaller then than it is now). For Lafite the Rothschilds had paid as much as for all these three put together, and very nearly as much again: here was a record indeed.

The furniture of the château itself, and its cellar of fine wines—great years not only of Lafite—were reserved by the Vanlerberghe heirs and sold separately, at the property, in November.

This wine sale developed into a duel between a Paris and a Bordeaux restaurateur for the finest Lafites, which ranged from a couple of bottles of the 1797 Lafite—the first château-bottled year—by way of eleven bottles of 1811, the 'comet' year, to the already famous 1864. Eventually the cream of the collection went to M. Gremailly, proprietor of the Hotel des Princes et de la Paix at Bordeaux, with M. Delhomme, of the Paris Café Anglais as his under-bidder for most of the lots. The cheapest of the old wines was the 1826, which went for the same price as the recent, and not too highly regarded 1863—seven francs a bottle. The eleven bottles of the 'comet' wine went for 121 francs a bottle—

with the franc then at twenty-five to the pound, and the extra five per cent commission charged to buyers, more than £5 a bottle, a phenomenal price for those days.

Other prices per bottle, according to Bertall, were:

1798	—	16 francs
1815	—	31 ,,
1823	—	60 ,,
1825	—	36 ,,
1834	—	70 ,,
1846	—	27 ,,
1848	—	65 ,,
1858	—	36 ,,

Some must have been bought back by the Rothschilds, then or later, for all the great years of Lafite sold at this auction are now represented in the collection at the château itself.

* * *

By this time, though, the Baron James was dead. As has already been suggested, it is very doubtful whether he had ever visited Lafite before the sale. What would have taken him there before it was known to be in the market, by which time he was already a sick old man? And it is highly improbable that he was fit enough for what was still in those days an arduous journey, in the few weeks between the purchase and his death.

So Lafite became the joint property, in equal parts, of James's three surviving sons: Alphonse, Gustave and Edmond. By the Jewish laws of inheritance, which Rothschilds take with them wherever they go, women inherit nothing; their only sister Charlotte came in for no part of the Lafite property and neither, therefore, did her husband, Nathaniel, the owner of Mouton.[7]

But Jews are dutiful sons, and if James's widow, the Baroness

[7] There has never been any overlapping of family ownership between Mouton and Lafite, and Nathaniel's great-grandson, Baron Phillipe, the present owner of Mouton, tells me that there was never any foundation for the story, current immediately after the war, and repeated in Warner Allen's *Natural Red Wines* (1951) that it had been intended then that he should take an active interest in the production of Lafite. There were young Rothschilds of the direct Lafite line to do that, as we shall see.

Betty, had no claim in Jewish law to Lafite there is no doubt that in the family she was regarded as having at least as much moral right to it as anyone. She seems to have spent much of her early widowhood there—there is still some of her deeply black-edged mourning writing paper and envelopes in the little summer parlour—and much, perhaps most, of the furniture and fabrics that we see in the reception rooms now are what the Baroness Betty brought from the great family château at Ferriéres to replace those sold at the wine and furniture sale held at Lafite in November 1868. She liked the house and, absurdly modest though its accommodation was compared with the Rothschild palaces available to her, she may well have visited it fairly regularly, if not frequently, until her death in 1886.

*   *   *

If, as I have suggested, it was James's three sons, Alphonse, Gustave and Edmond, who had pushed him into buying Lafite, they seem, nevertheless, to have spent little time there, though Edmond was interested in wine-growing, and helped the Russian Jews who had fled from the pogroms of the 1880s to establish vineyards in Palestine—the origin of Israel's present flourishing wine-growing industry.

For the next couple of years they all, as partners in the bank, had much else to think about, and Alphonse, the head of the firm and of the family, in particular: he helped Jules Favre to negotiate with Bismarck the terms of the Franco-Prussian peace treaty of 1871, and it was the Rothschild bank, with Alphonse its most active partner, that underwrote and raised—two years before the due date—the indemnity exacted by the Prussians, which many, among them the Crown Prince of Prussia himself, had thought too vast to be raised at all.

There were two coincidences about this peace treaty in which the house of Rothschild had had a hand (and not only the French house: the London bank had also been involved, and the pigeon post between Rothschilds at Rue Laffitte and Rothschilds at New Court is said to have been constantly ahead of the news reaching Prussian headquarters).

For one thing, it was signed eventually at Frankfurt, whence the Rothschilds had sprung, and its preliminaries, moreover, were negotiated largely at Ferrières, the Rothschild mansion eight miles from Versailles, which had been requisitioned as head-quarters for the King of Prussia, Bismarck and von Moltke during the siege of Paris.

If seven years is not too long to wait for such a thing, it can even be claimed that there was to be a third coincidence linking Bismarck with the French Rothschilds and their wine.

In 1877, Disraeli, almost seventy-three, was suffering from Bright's disease, bronchitis and asthma, and was acutely depressed, writing gloomily to Lady Bradford about resigning the premiership. A new physician, Dr Kidd, a homoeopath, was brought in, who pronounced that Disraeli's condition was aggravated by the nostrums of previous doctors: ipecacuanha for his asthma, some iron compound for debility, and port. The ipecacuanha made him feel sick; the iron gave him a headache, and the port accentuated a tendency to gout. Dr Kidd substituted potassium iodide for the iron and the ipecacuanha and, according to his latest biographer,[8] 'also wisely forbade port and prescribed instead "the finest Château Lafite"—a change which suited Disraeli, who disliked port but was devoted to claret'.

In not much more than six months—in June 1878,—Disraeli was 'the lion of the Congress' at Berlin. According to Mr Robert Blake, his 'vitality was astounding. The social life at Berlin . . . would have been enough to exhaust most men . . .' And then there were the endless meetings, the daily reports to Queen Victoria 'in his most scintillating vein, packed with vivid pictures, incisive pen portraits and amusing stories. Nor, it need scarcely be said, did his correspondence with Lady Bradford and Lady Chesterfield ever flag.'

Little wonder that Bismarck exclaimed, '*Der alte Jude, das ist der Mann!*' There is no reason to suppose that Bismarck knew that Disraeli's tonic was the wine grown by the Baron Alphonse who had stood up to his brusqueries at Ferrières, and it is a pity that

[8] Robert Blake, *Disraeli*, New York 1966.

that other *alte Jude*, Baron James, did not live to know that 'the finest Château Lafite' had had something to do with the amazing septuagenarian's vitality.

*   *   *

King Wilhelm said that kings could not afford Ferrières: 'it could only belong to a Rothschild!' He would not use anything so splendid himself as the Baron Alphonse's bedroom and ordered that nothing must be touched—not the pictures in the saloons, nor the game in the park, nor the wine in the cellars.

There is still a copy at Ferrières of the steward's report to Baron Alphonse of his having refused to serve Bismarck with any of the family's wine, and of their having to do so against payment. Bismarck, in fact, behaved badly: he shot the Ferrières pheasants in spite of his master's edict, and the Prussian Crown Prince noted in his diary that he behaved with 'monstrous *brusquerie* and intentional rudeness', especially to Baron Alphonse, who addressed him in French.

This too, though, was arrogance on the part of Baron Alphonse, whose father and mother had been German-born, and had never lost their guttural accents, and whose German uncle and cousins Bismarck had known well. But it provided an admirable precedent for Alphonse's great-nephew, Baron Elie, who taken prisoner by the Germans at the very beginning of the 1939-45 war, when he was only twenty-two, would stubbornly refuse to answer his name at the prison-camp roll call if it was pronounced in the German way, with a long 'o', saying that he was a French officer and a Frenchman, and recognized only the French pronunciation.

Baron Elie is one of the five cousins (two of them brothers) who are now the joint owners of Lafite—four great-grandsons of Baron James, together with Mrs 'Jimmy' de Rothschild, widow of the grandson who became an English Liberal M.P., and whose share in this family property she has inherited by family agreement, though Jewish tradition would have ordained otherwise.

It is best, perhaps, to explain it by means of a simplified tree:

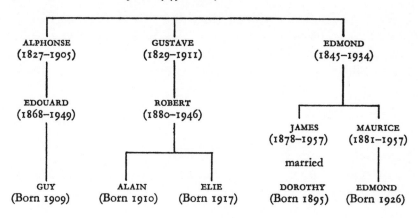

JAMES (1792–1868)

ALPHONSE (1827–1905) — GUSTAVE (1829–1911) — EDMOND (1845–1934)

EDOUARD (1868–1949) — ROBERT (1880–1946)

JAMES (1878–1957)   MAURICE (1881–1957)

married

GUY (Born 1909)   ALAIN (Born 1910)   ELIE (Born 1917)   DOROTHY (Born 1895)   EDMOND (Born 1926)

The five named in the bottom row are the present owners of Lafite, which is divided into six shares, of which Baron Guy as the head of the family owns two, the others one each.

But it is Baron Elie to whom Baron Guy handed control of the property after the war, when much had to be done to restore the prestige of Lafite and the moral of its workers, not only because of the years of German occupation, but the previous years of bad vintages and dwindling markets—the wretched decade of the nineteen-thirties, when poor vintages coincided with the aftermath of the Wall Street crash, so that all the great claret houses were in a poor way when war broke out, including Lafite.

When Baron Elie took over Lafite, he was not yet out of his twenties—'probably the fiercest, most imperious family member since the first Lord Rothschild', writes Mr Frederic Morton in his *The Rothschilds: A family portrait*. He is still, at just over fifty, imperious in his manner and dashing in his pleasures—a crack shot and a polo player of international class. There is no doubt that he galvanized Lafite, startling and delighting the staff there by his ability both to praise and to berate them in a Médocain accent.

He took over Lafite in 1946, with the stern warning from his cousin Guy that even Rothschilds, these days, could not go on losing money over even so marginal a property as Lafite, and that unless it was put upon an economic footing it might have to be sold. Baron Elie takes pleasure now in recalling that in 1948

Lafite paid its first dividend since the Rothschild purchase in 1868: two thousand francs (present day 'new' francs, that is) for each share—four thousand to cousin Guy. It must be the only Rothschild property that has taken eighty years to show a profit.

The salon rouge, with walls and upholstery in red damask. The portrait
over the Chinese cabinet is of Baron James as a young man

The Summer Parlour: the walls are painted a pale biscuit colour and
the whole scheme is suggestive of coolness

PLATE VII

The library: walls, curtains and upholstery are all in rich green

The dining room: pale duck-egg green and white walls setting off
the pink and blue dinner service

PLATE VIII

5. The House

Four of the village communes—perhaps the nearest English word is parish—that are each entitled to its own *appellation* within the wider one of Médoc or Haut-Médoc are vastly more important than the others. They are Margaux, St Julien, Pauillac and St Estèphe. Of these, Pauillac has the greatest claim to fame, and makes the least to-do about it.

Within its boundaries are no fewer than eighteen of the *crus classés* of the classification of 1855—St Julien has eleven, and St Estèphe five. True, Margaux (now that Cantenac, Soussans, Arsac and Labarde are included, as they were not in 1855) can claim as many as twenty-one of the classed growths, but only Pauillac can claim *two* of the first growths of the Médoc; Lafite and Latour, —and that is to say nothing of Mouton, which Mouton would not like, for it is quite the lordliest, quite the most famous of the second growths, and now commands the same price as most firsts. Margaux has only one first growth, Château Margaux itself, and the only other first growth, Haut Brion, is not in the Médoc at all, but in the commune of Pessac, in the Graves, on the other side of Bordeaux.

Drive out from Bordeaux along D2, the road that leads to the Pointe de Grave, at the very tip of the Médoc peninsula, running never more than a few hundred yards from the western shore of the Gironde, though hardly ever—because of trees and the slight undulations of the ground—with a view of the river, and you pass virtually all the great châteaux of the region.

Actually, the road begins five miles from the city, with a turning to the right off D1, which is signposted to Lesparre, and runs through the very middle of the Médoc, with hardly a view of any serious vineyard. But take the right turn that is signposted Pauillac, and in another five miles the first noble vines appear: those of La Lagune, and then of Cantemerle. Another four or five, and you enter the tiny village of Margaux, to be greeted by the boast, in huge letters, and flanked by a coat-of-arms, painted on the wall that turns at an angle to face the motorist driving from Bordeaux:

MARGAUX
VINS ROUGES LES PLUS
CELEBRES DU MONDE

Five miles or so further on, and you come upon St Julien, smaller even than the village of Margaux, but more peremptory, its signboard demanding, in half-a-dozen colours and as many styles of lettering:

PASSANTS!
VOUS ENTREZ SUR L'ANTIQUE ET CELEBRE
CRU DE ST JULIEN:
SALUEZ

—following up this modest greeting with a metal simulacrum of a claret bottle, a couple of dozen feet high, the most vulgar thing in the Médoc, standing in a vineyard by the side of the road, and bearing the label: 'Grand Vin de St Julien: Médoc.'

Even little St Estèphe, farthest-flung of the Haut-Médoc communes, beyond Pauillac, paints a whole house-end in the middle of the village with a map showing every vineyard in the commune, *bourgeois* as well as *classé*, and an invitation to the village wine-museum, open seven days a week, and concerned only with the wines of St Estèphe. I have never gone into this museum but to find myself alone (the village itself seems usually to be deserted, save when some modest local bicycle race goes that way), and I cannot believe that throughout the year it averages more than a couple of visitors a day to listen to its tape-recorded lecture.

None of these three villages, for all the splendour of its name upon a wine list, is substantial enough for even the smallest entry in the *Guide Michelin*, but Pauillac, between St Julien and St Estèphe, is a sizeable little town of some six thousand people. Unlike the others, too, (and all the other villages of the Médoc, until you reach the very tip of the peninsula, at Verdon), in being actually on the riverside, to which it presents a quiet, rather shabby but dignified frontage largely Empire in style, it has a couple of jetties and is the pick-up point for the river pilots that take big ships up to Bordeaux.

As a port, indeed, Pauillac has earned its modest mentions in the French history books. It was from here, in 1777, that the young Lafayette set sail for America in the *Victoire*, and in 1815 the duchesse d'Angoulême (Madame Royal, or 'the orphan of the Temple') daughter of the guillotined Louis XVI and Marie-Antoinette, having failed to raise Bordeaux for her cousin Louis XVIII during Napoleon's Hundred Days, slipped away to England from Pauillac in the *Wanderer*.

Pauillac is now the port for a small Shell refinery, and now, too, that a sailing school for young people has been set up there— one of the many such admirable enterprises sponsored by the Ministere de la Jeunesse et des Sports—it is becoming in a small way something of a weekend resort and a dinghy-sailing centre, so that what were the simplest of shops and the humblest of village inns only a very few years ago are now smartening themselves up, and the cafés are doing a roaring trade. One, of course, is the Café du Sport, but another is the Café du Yachting.

The process of change is being accelerated, too, by the growing prosperity and sophistication of what used to be a simple peasantry. For it is not only tourists and travelling wine-merchants and undergraduate yachtsmen who patronize Pauillac's new hair-dressing parlours and scent shops and self-service stores, but also the wives and daughters of *vignerons* and cellarmen, and the small peasant farmers who, making sure that their own grapes are gathered before those of their lordlier neighbours, turn up at the

Latour or the Lafite or the Mouton *vendange* in their Peugeots and Simcas and Citroëns *deux chevaux*.

But in spite of all this growing grandeur, and in spite of the renown of its wines, Pauillac counters the proud blazonings of the three tiny villages that are its rivals with nothing more than a faded little tin plaque at the entrance to the town, speckled with the rust of long neglect, and not a tenth the size of any of the others, to carry its claim, at least as justified as Margaux's, but hardly noticeable, let alone readable:

PAUILLAC
SES VINS LES PREMIERS DU MONDE

And its wine museum on the river front (housed in a room of the Château Grand Puy Ducasse, the vineyards of which are on the very edge of the town and of the Shell refinery, which seems to do them no harm), magnanimously concerns itself not with the wines of Pauillac only but with the whole of the Médoc: Pauillac is the headquarters of the Commanderie du Bontemps.

The two great first-growth clarets of Pauillac are as dignified in their reticence as is Pauillac itself.

Neither for Château Lafite nor for Château Latour the great placards and wall-painted pronouncements along the road from Bordeaux that advertise the name of M. Alexis Lichine at least as vociferously as those of his Château Lascombes and his Château Prieuré, or the great black-and-white boards that hold up the name and the trade-mark of Château Beychevelle to every passing motorist. Not even the flags and the flowers of Château Palmer, pretty as they are.

Pointing to each is simply the standard signpost of the region, such as there is for every château, and no more, except that Lafite allows itself the smallest practicable name-boards—you do not notice them if you drive quickly past—on such of its vineyards as might be confused with those of Mouton, which in some parts dovetail with Lafite's.

There is only a very small house at Latour, and the house at Lafite is not open to the public, as the *chais* are, nor does it hold exhibitions of paintings, as Lascombes does from May to October every year, or house such treasures as the works of art—jewellery and porcelain, silver and gold plate, antiques and antiquities,—as are displayed to the public in the museum at Mouton. Even the Lafite *chais*, open as they are to the public, are not dramatized as is the one at Mouton, with its coat-of-arms, and its clever lighting.

*　　*　　*

Château Lafite itself stands back a little from the road D2, just beyond Pauillac and the little village of Le Pouyalet as you drive north from Bordeaux, and the passing motorist, unless he is looking out for it, gets only a brief glimpse before it is hidden again by its trees, or lost among its outbuildings.

Even on Saturday and Sunday evenings in the summer, when it is floodlit, it is as a contribution to the landscape only, not as an advertising device, for there is nothing to indicate that this is Château Lafite. Then, too, the glimpse of it has gone almost before the family driving back to Bordeaux after its day at the sea—at Soulac on the Atlantic or at Le Verdon on the Gironde or over the ferry to Royan—has realized that it is upon it. But there is one point, and on a summer's evening it is worth stopping the car to walk along and find it, where there is a narrow gap in a line of weeping willows by the road, through which the château, with its round tower and its pepper-pot, framed in the foreground by the willows and then, farther back, by its own trees and the terrace balustrade, looks like an illustration for a Perrault fairy-story (Plate V). All the more so when, as I last saw it, there is a star above, and the slenderest of new moons.

By the roadside, the property is edged by a narrow little brook, fringed by the weeping willows I have mentioned. Where it meets the entrance gate there is a square, stone-flagged artificial pool, where a few of the oldest village women from Le Pouyalet still come, when the weather is clement, to do their family washing, for the water is so pure, and village custom in France dies so hard. The spring that feeds the pool, in a paddock a hundred yards or so from the road, lies under an eighteenth-century open pavilion, supported by columns—like a building, says the Baroness Liliane, in a Hubert Robert painting.

A not very regular, not especially stately, but pretty avenue of elms and other trees leads up to the long, low *chai*, and then turns, past meadow and kitchen garden and paddock, to the south side of the house, where the entrance is, and the low flanking terrace of workers' cottages. The late-seventeenth-century balustrade of the terrace, and the square pillars that hold the wrought-iron entrance gates, are of sandstone, ranging in colour from the palest of grey to an even paler yellow, flaking with age, and flecked a little with the black and the gold of lichen. It is not unlike the stone of Cotswold manors and Oxford quadrangles.

Look hard, and tap with your fingernails at the railings, for they are not what they seem. It is the same at the back of the house, where the ornamental gateway that leads to the woodland pleasaunce is called La Garenne, the warren: all the railing verticals save those of the main gateway itself, to the south of the front lawns, are of wood, painted black and fashioned into spikes to resemble the iron stays and the horizontals. The Baroness believes that the original iron was taken away almost a century before the Rothschilds ever came here, to be fashioned into arms for the first ragged armies of the young Republic.

Balustrade and pillars seem to have been meant for a bigger and a grander house, for the château itself, far from being a château in the sense in which one speaks of a château of the Loire, or even as the splendid Château Beychevelle is, with its spreading grounds, or the elegantly-porticoed Château Margaux, is more of a sizeable manor-house, or *gentilhommière*, relatively modest in its size, and very modest in its pretensions.

It stands among small lawns—one bordered with roses, inside another border of lavender; one with a couple of fine magnolias and a splendid cedar.

Except for its height, the front door might be that almost of a country cottage—narrow, hung with wistaria, tucked into the corner formed by the southern side of the house and the kitchen. Too modest, even, to have steps to it, which the French find odd, indeed: a gentleman's threshold should not be flush with his drive.

The east front, with its four tall French windows and four narrower windows above, looks out over paddock and kitchen garden and willows, across the D2 road to a huddle of farm buildings, some of its own outlying vineyards, and a glimpse of the tops of the oil tanks at the Shell refinery at Pauillac. And at just one point, if you know where to look, there is a little notch in the trees perhaps a little to the north of east, where you can see as much of the Gironde as the half-moon on your little finger-nail. That is if the sun catches the water, to turn it into silver-grey; or if there is a ship there, to show a red or a yellow funnel growing incongruously out of the bosky green. It is said that for a vineyard of the Médoc to be truly great, its vines must see the river, and that those of all the greatest growths do so, but some of the vines of Lafite and some of its visitors see no more of it than this, and some are still looking for it.

The house is built of the same stone as the balustrade, but only the chimney-stacks, the pepper-pot clock-tower and the walls at the back reveal it. The façade and its great round tower (Plate VI) have been rendered with plaster and painted, in the manner of the south, so that they display the picturesquely stained and tex-tured buff and ochre surface that one sees in Florence and in Rome on an architectural profile that could not be more charac-teristically French.

It was suggested by the late Denise Bourdet in her charming booklet on Lafite that the château's three towers—the dominating round tower with its conical slate roof; the tiny pepper-pot, which is oval in section, and not round; and the square tower at the back—are all of different dates. It seems to me more likely that the pepper-pot and the square tower are contemporaries, as the treatment of their windows is identical, and neither seems more weather-worn than the other. These two towers were, I think, at the corners of the original house—the lower part of the pepper-pot, certainly, has been obscured by the addition of the kitchen wing, itself of considerable age.

The east front is obviously later than these two towers, and the round tower at its northern end is as obviously much earlier. This tower, with its medieval conical roof,—there is a legend that Eleanor of Aquitaine once slept in it—makes a pleasingly asymmetrical composition with the front of the house. The elabor-ate gable-end denies itself a northern curlicue to accommodate

the tower, and the upper and the lower windows at this end
are narrower than the others, as though the architect had for-
gotten altogether to allow for the tower, and the builders had to
squeeze them in as best they could.

However that may be, all is happily pulled together by colour
and by texture, by the white-painted shutters, and by the wistaria
on the south side, the climbing roses on the round tower, and the
hydrangeas at its base. One would not have it otherwise.

The kitchen wing on the south may well have been an addition
too, as I have suggested, but a very early one, for the kitchen itself, no longer used, is vast, still with its spit and enormous
bread-oven, and with deeply worn flagstones. Nowadays this
wing provides accommodation for a gardener and his wife, with
a small modern kitchen; a guest-room; and an office and a four-
bedroomed flat for the *régisseur*.

There is another kitchen, smaller, but also of some age, on
the farther side of the house, with a hatch to the dining-room.

*   *   *

Like the front door itself, the tiled entrance-hall, too, is small—
too small, indeed, to show off as it should be shown the massively
handsome, squarely self-confident, seventeenth-century stone
staircase which, like the terrace, seems to have been made for a
bigger house. The urns at the corners of the balustrade would be
charming were it not that when the Germans were in occupation
they plastered them over—one cannot imagine why—with a hard
shiny cream paint that nobody has since been able to remove
for fear of damaging the surface of the stone beneath.

The Germans did other odd things here—not destructive, but
unaccountable, such as plastering the lower part of the pretty
painted walls in the summer parlour. But the Rothschilds owe
two things at any rate to the Germans at Lafite: they put in
electricity and modern plumbing. (Late in 1967, when the family's
private bedroom accommodation was being extended, I was just
in time to see, before they were removed, the row of showers
that the Germans had installed, in a sort of ablution block for
other ranks.)

Other pieces of other periods have settled down happily in the hall—the high, early rococo, eighteenth-century porcelain stove for instance, the work, it is thought, of an itinerant Italian craftsman; a tall eighteenth-century press from Bordeaux, and, at the first turn of the stairs, the Victorian marble bust of Nathan Rothschild, eldest of the five original Rothschild brothers, as James, the purchaser of Lafite, was the youngest. It was James's widow, the Baroness Betty, who bought, and brought here, the great swirlingly allegorical paintings that hang above the staircase—cartoons for eighteenth-century tapestries.

Apart from the hall and the tiny 'bureau de Baron Elie'—a square room, although it is actually the ground floor of the round tower, and with space for little more than a chair, a table, and a sofa—there are only four ground-floor rooms. (There is a number of bedrooms for guests and for the occasional visits by the family, so necessarily redesigned and redecorated that they need not concern us here: they are, of course, charming, but they are not the old Lafite. In any case, they are private apartments.)

None of the ground-floor rooms is bigger than one would normally find in a sizeable English country house; none is at all deliberately imposing; none has any special treasures in the way of works of art; yet all have the charm of rooms that are true to their period without self-consciousness, and all are patently Rothschild rooms, though of the cosiest and most *bourgeois* sort.

By the time that James bought Lafite, Rothschilds were lording it with the lordliest in London and Paris and Vienna, cramming and ornamenting vast palaces in Buckinghamshire and the Ile de France and on the Prinzeugenstrasse with what Mr Osbert Lancaster has described as 'le style Rothschild', yet here, in the Médoc, nothing is more ambitious, more ostentatious, than any comfortably-off country gentleman, devoted to his vines, his kitchen-garden and his pocket-handkerchief lawns, might reasonably provide so as to be able to entertain his fellow wine-growing neighbours decently to dinner, and so that his wife and the other ladies might be comfortable while he and their husbands finished their claret.

Which repository that claret would have come from, in the early Rothschild days at Lafite, I do not know. Today, unless it is a real museum piece that is chosen, the fine wine that Baron

Elie and the Baroness serve to their guests comes not from the little *caveau* in the château, reached from a door in the hall, under the great staircase, but from the enormously bigger *cave* that opens from the *cave de la troisième année*, under the complex of out-buildings in the courtyard.

The *caveau* is a small vaulted cellar that is primarily—almost entirely—a museum. Almost every year of Lafite is represented here by one, two or up to six bottles (more of the later vintages), from the classic 1797, the first château-bottled Lafite, down (so far) to 1914, along with some rare old vintages of Latour, Mouton, the Léovilles and Gruaud-Larose. These wines belong jointly to the five owners of Lafite, though there are a few pre-1914 bottles that are the personal property of each of the proprietors, but these, too, are regarded more as curiosities than as beverages. All told, there are about 1500 bottles here; they are recorked every eight to ten years or so—this was last done in 1959, and is due to be done again.

In the great *cave* (Plate XIII), on the other hand, there are getting on for twenty times as many bottles, dating back only to 1910—25,000 or thereabouts, added to every year, and recorked every twenty to twenty-five—the *réserve des propriétaires*, for drinking.

It was from here, for instance, that I have seen a bottle of the 1918 Lafite brought for a family luncheon at the château. The long corridors, lined with metal racks, heavily cobwebbed, hold not only bottles but magnums (double bottles), double magnums, jeroboams (six bottles), and the great *impériale* of Bordeaux, which holds eight bottles, or six litres. Six litres of the Lafite of a great year, in one bottle, justifies so resounding a title.

*   *   *

The biggest of the reception rooms, the Salon Rouge (Plate VII a), not much bigger than the drawing-room of an English vicarage, opens off the hall, and takes up the south-east corner, with windows on two sides. The walls are hung with, and the chairs and sofas are buttoned into, red damask. All is kept just so: when the red damask of the pretty little love-seat became worn at the arms and at the bend of the seats sooner than any other piece—

for everyone who sees it must sit in it—the Baroness had a copy woven to recover it, just as she had net curtains made to precisely the same pattern as the originals, with their vine-leaf and grape motif.

This design picks up the motif of the stone chimney-breast, which is of the eighteenth century, as are the two pretty plaster figures, more than life-size, one of a boy with a garland, one of a girl with a flower-basket, in the corner niches. But these, like the painted panel above the door leading to the next room, serve only to set off the drawing-room's predominantly Second Empire feeling and atmosphere.

Paintings and a bust portray four of the five Rothschild brothers who sallied out from Frankfurt—or, rather, three who set out and one who stayed, for there, between chubby, snub-nosed, thick-lipped Nathan of London and the elegant Salomon of Vienna, with his walking-stick, is Amschel of Frankfurt, the map of Germany behind him and a plan in his hand of the *Eisen-Bahn zwischen Wien*.... The portraits are copies of originals that are in Paris.

There is no portrait, alas, of Carl of Naples, but there is both a picture here of James, painted when he was young and lively-looking, and a marble bust of him on the chimney-piece, showing him middle-aged and heavily whiskered, looking out over the disarmingly sentimental Second Empire needlework firescreen, facing which is a giant Second Empire pouffe, upholstered in the same buttoned red damask as all else.

The other pictures are nineteenth-century Dutch seascapes; there are nineteenth-century photographs and portrait-drawings on the pretty little French piano; and there is nineteenth-century Bohemian red glass on this small table and on that, none the less charming for being of neither artistic merit nor intrinsic value, but wholly in the idiom of the room.

Between the two windows that face east, though, is a three-drawer mahogany-and-brass writing table, its leather top worn, torn and shabby. This was brought by Baron Alphonse, James's eldest son, from the family mansion at Ferrières, which (as already mentioned) was requisitioned in 1870 by Wilhelm of Prussia, General von Moltke and Bismarck during the siege of Paris, and is the one at which Bismarck dictated to Jules Favre the draft terms of what was to be the Treaty of Frankfurt.

Various stories are told to account for the great ink-stain on its top. Baron Alphonse, who had succeeded James as head of the family and the bank barely a couple of years before, was present at the negotiations, helping to guarantee food supplies to beleaguered Paris, and underwriting the payment of the vast indemnity that was being demanded: some say that it was his bland refusal to speak German—this grandson of the Frankfurt ghetto —that made Bismarck thump the table with his fist, and spill the ink; some that it was his equally bland assurance that the money was an easy matter.

But the present family subscribe to none of these stories about the stain. I am not sure, even, that every Rothschild is positive that it is indubitably the desk at which Bismarck sat, though there is some support for the belief. There is an account, for instance, of a visit paid to Lafite in 1888 by members of a horticultural congress meeting in Bordeaux, who were shown the desk, and told its history: I cannot believe that in less than twenty years a false legend had been created around this piece of furniture.

It is odd now to read the account written by the official chronicler of the congress's trip down the Gironde in the steamer *Magicienne*:

'. . . it was not without a horrible contraction of the heart that we contemplated the already famous and historic table . . . saturated with the saddest and the bloodiest memories.

'Yes, it is on this wretched piece of furniture that the Arminius of our time, the pitiless Iron Chancellor, after having cried into the face of terrified Europe a new "Vae Victis!" imposed his draconian laws on our poor dear country, dying now, widowed and orphaned, overwhelmed by numbers, but unconquered, covered with wounds and cruelly dismembered, a foot on her throat, shamefully ransomed and outrageously violated. One day that will all be washed out . . .'

If he could have lived to see German prisoners working in the Lafite vineyards in 1945, perhaps he would have felt that honour had been satisfied.

What I find much more moving about the Bismarck desk is

that as I sat at it myself writing the notes for this chapter, I looked in the middle drawer for more paper and came, instead, upon the order of service for the *barmitzvah* (confirmation) celebrations at the Great Synagogue, London, in October 1964, of one of the youngest of the English Rothschilds, who are remote cousins,—the family is still a very united one, and still stubbornly Jewish.

Opening out from this main drawing-room is the one remaining eighteenth-century room in the house—the little *salon d'été*, or summer parlour (Plate VIII b), facing east, and decorated in cool colours, with *grisaille* ovals above the doors, and vases and swags and sprigs of flowers painted on the light-buff painted walls. This is what the other reception rooms must have looked like before Baron James's widow refurnished them, in the last years of the Second Empire and the first of the Third Republic. The links between the centuries are the chimney-breast in the *salon rouge*, and its plaster figures.

Here, in the pretty little parlour, the Louis Seize chairs are covered in the needlework of the period, now pleasantly faded; there is marquetry furniture; but the inevitable nineteenth-century family note is struck by yellowing photographs—the two groups of very small ones, Polyfotos of the period, portray a heavy Rothschild swell of the 1860s in deliberately comic attitudes: in one he poses as a mesmerist[1]—and, on a small writing-table, a rack holding the heavily black-edged and funereally coronetted mourning stationery on which the Baroness Betty acknowledged condolences on the death of the uncle-husband who had bought Lafite and never lived there—paper and envelopes that have long outlived the bereaved, as well as the dear departed.

[1] One cannot be sure, but I think that this may very well be Salomon, who died in 1864 at the age of twenty-nine, the only son of James and Betty, who did not live to see the Lafite purchase. The photographs resemble those I have seen of him, and it seems probable that his mother would have kept photographs of the one son who had died—and who had been the family scapegrace. For the comic postures are in character, and strengthen me in my guess. He was always in trouble in Paris ('he was less addicted to steady work and habits of business than his brothers', wrote his cousin, Lady Battersea), and was banished by his father, first to Frankfurt and then to New York, where he was blackballed by the New York Club as being 'immoderately given to lewd talk and nude photographs'.

What earns the grand title of library (Plate VIII a) for the little room next to the dining-room, furnished with grained woodwork and green damask, is a pair, simply, of glass-fronted bookcases, five feet high and less than that wide, darkly varnished and heavily inlaid, filled with standard sets, leather-bound, of Balzac and Dumas, Saint-Simon and Madame de Staël, all bearing the Baron James's heraldic bookplate and, surprisingly, a set of Gothic horror novels—*The Monk, The Mysteries of Udolpho*, and the like—printed in English but published in Paris; and the pretty eighteenth-century Cooks' pocket edition of English poets and novelists. I doubt whether these were James's, and fancy they have been added since his time, to fill the shelves.

Four paintings here show various Rothschild children of the middle of the last century—some babies, some ten or twelve years old or so: James's grandchildren or perhaps even his younger children, for there was twenty years between his eldest and his youngest. There are linen trousers and tartan sashes, lace collars and muslin frocks: it was an appealing period for child portraits.

And there is one painting of a woman, with the head of a tragedy queen and a fist full of paintbrushes—a Rothschild probably; certainly a Jewess. It is signed with the improbable name of Emma Goggiotti Richards and, as a painting, has no distinction whatsoever, but the face has more than enough: some of the Rothschild women must have been tigresses.

*　　　*　　　*

Most austere, though by no means the least pretty, of the ground-floor rooms is the dining-room (Plate VIII b), which was once dining-room dark brown, but which the Baroness has had painted in pale duck-egg green and white, setting off and being set off by the pink-and-blue dinner service, with its Rothschild monogram and coronet, also in pink and blue. This is of simple Bordeaux ware. The factory was set up by the English potter, D. Johnson (not to be confused with the wine-shipper, Johnston), in the 1830s after the Bordeaux painted faïence industry had been ruined by the Revolution; it made earthenware after the English method and was carried on after his death by Viellard. The Lafite service dates from the Viellard period. The same factory produced a series of views of the châteaux of the Médoc now much sought after (Plate XVI a).

The service is pretty but countrified, exactly suitable for the modest country house in which it is used, as are the country-made, round-backed mahogany chairs, which if they were German one would call Biedermayer, but are of the 1820s or thereabouts, and came from Poitou.

The bust of James on the chimney-piece here is bigger than that in the drawing-room, and there are more Rothschild portraits on the walls. But there is no piece of furniture here, no porcelain, no painting, one half so fine even of its own kind, far less so absolutely aristocratic, as any of the bottles of Lafite that have been passed round this table by Baron James's descendants.

Perfection here has the simplest of settings.

6. Interlude

MANY tales have been, and are still being, told in Bordeaux by those eager, after the war, to curry favour with the returning Rothschilds—even, in the past, by those anxious to offset charges of collaboration—about their having helped to save Lafite or, more particularly, its collection of wines from the Germans. There are also stories about the senior German officer in Bordeaux, in civilian life a distinguished wine-shipper, with many friends in the Bordeaux wine trade—that he warned the officers billeted at Lafite and at Mouton that in the cellars there were the finest wines in France; that Marshal Goering would certainly want them for his own collection; and that lesser fry would do well to keep their hands off them.

All this is as may be. Some are dead who could tell the truth of the matter, or might not tell it if they were alive. Some still alive genuinely find it difficult now, after a quarter of a century, to disentangle fact from wistful fantasy; what they once knew from what they have since been told.

It may well be that there were those—German as well as French—who were ready to do a good turn to a Jewish family some of the members of which were now elderly exiles, some with the Free French, some in German prison camps. But as it turned out, the property was kept intact for them, however unintentionally, by the Vichy government.

Baron Robert, Elie's father, was the last of a number of Rothschilds of his generation—he was sixty—to get out of France through Lafite. He and his wife and daughters, some infant

An old master and a young wine: the
former *maître de chai*

rges Revelle, the present *maître
de chai*

PLATE IX

The great fermenting vats of Bosnian oak in the *cuvier*

PLATE X

grandchildren, and Elie's fiancée, Liliane Fould-Springer,[1] spent a few days there before he, with most of the party, (Mlle Fould-Springer escaped into Spain), caught the last ship to leave the Pointe de Grave in 1940.

Mme Gaby Faux, then the Lafite book-keeper and now retired, who was left in charge of the family's effects at Lafite, is still moved when she tells of the trouble that Baron Robert went to in leaving cash and valuables with her to ensure that servants and pensioners should not, if he could help it, be left penniless through any German or Vichy blocking of Rothschild bank accounts.

His sons, Alain and Elie, who had been reserve officers in a French cavalry regiment, had both been taken prisoner in the early days of the war, in the fighting on the Maginot Line; his nephew, Guy, escaped through Dunkirk, reached New York in 1941, and eventually (after being torpedoed in the Atlantic) joined de Gaulle's staff.

Meanwhile, though, after the escape of Baron Robert and his family, and before the arrival only a week or so later of the fifty or so German officers and men—some from the Judge Advocate General's department, together with a few light anti-aircraft gunners—who were to be billeted on the château for nearly four years, Mme Faux had the remarkable collection of some two thousand bottles of old wine moved from the *caveau* in the château, (which I have described in Chapter 5). There it could not but have been discovered, for its door is in the front hall, but Mme Faux had it stealthily moved to one of the old, remoter cellar passages where it did, it seems, remain unnoticed, certainly undisturbed, throughout the war.

She then set to, and by skilful juggling with names and dates in her records, sitting up all of several nights to do it, transferred the ownership of most of the other, bigger cellars of fine wines, from the older generation of Rothschilds (Edmond, Robert and Maurice—who had escaped from France, and thus, it was already to be expected, would forfeit French citizenship), to the brothers Alain and Elie, now prisoners-of-war, whose property, they felt

---

[1] It is interesting that the Baroness Elie is a kinswoman of the family, Fould—now Achille-Fould—that owns Château Beychevelle. The Achille Fould of the Second Empire was a banking rival of the Rothschilds.

safe in assuming, would be under some sort of protection from Hague or Geneva conventions.

It may be that this act of devotion by a loyal servant saved the two collections of fine wines; it may be that, however farsighted, it was unnecessary. It was some time before the ownership of Lafite and its contents was legally decided, but the Germans in possession behaved correctly enough in the meantime, save for writing 'JUDE!' on the marble bust of Nathan that now stands at the turn of the stairs, and throwing it into the backyard. Whether they would have respected the contents of the *caveau*, that lay just beyond and below the quite obvious door in the front hall if it had not then been empty, we cannot now know, but Baron Elie and the Baroness speak gratefully of Mme Faux to this day.

The formalities of the situation were this. On July 23, 1940, as expected and widely rumoured, Marshal Pétain signed a decree declaring that all French citizens who had left metropolitan French territory between May 10 and June 30 of that year, were to be regarded as having renounced French nationality, and their property as having been forfeited to the French state. Among them, of course, were *'les trois juifs déchus de leur nationalité'*— Edmond, Robert and Maurice de Rothschild, described as *'ennemis indesirables'*, along with their fellow owner of Lafite, James ('Jimmy') who was a naturalized Englishman.

So that when, in 1942, the occupying power claimed Lafite, on the grounds that one of its owners was James de Rothschild, an Englishman, the Vichy government's custodian of enemy property (or his deputy) deposed before Maître Jacques Vialard, the notary-public at Pauillac, that the estate had been the property of the French government and state since the departure of Edmond, Robert and Maurice, and the Germans accepted this without quibble.

So much for the property itself, and for the fine wines in its cellars. As for the current wines, the pre-1940 wines had already been sold and were in the cellars of Bordeaux *négociants* and shippers. The 1940 and 1941—both very light and, by Lafite standards, undistinguished wines—were presumably sold for the benefit of the custodian of enemy property. (As late as May 1944, only a matter of days before the Allied landings in Normandy, letters were still being exchanged between one Vichy ministry and another about the proper allocation of moneys from the Rothschild properties.) The 1942, 1943 and 1944 wines were gathered and made as normally as possible, considering the shortage of labour and of chemical insecticides and the like, and were in cask until the Rothschild return.

In April 1942, although the Germans remained installed in the château, the property was expropriated to the Vichy Ministry of Agriculture, which took it over in November, along with Mouton and Mouton d'Armailhacq (now Mouton Baron Philippe), and ran courses on wine-growing and wine-making, fruit-growing and cooperage, practical work being conducted at all three, but most of the lectures being given at Lafite.

All this time, too, most of the pre-war senior staff of Lafite, former Rothschild employees, remained at their jobs—handicapped, of course, by wartime shortage of labour.

Mme Faux had her living quarters in the servants' wing of the château, and went on with her book-keeping, while continuing to watch loyally over the family's interests. She rescued the bust of Nathan that the Germans had defaced and flung out, and kept it, along with the bust of Baron James that is now on the chimney-piece in the salon, and various other bibelots that she thought might arouse anti-Semitic spite, in her own apartments, which the Germans respected most punctiliously. Whether they would have done so had they known that in her bathroom was a great box containing the precious and sacred silver ornaments that were used to bedeck the scrolls of the law in the Great Synagogue of Paris in the Rue de la Victoire is a matter for conjecture. Baron Robert had been its President, and had been asked to take them with him to Lafite for safe-keeping. They are now back at the Rue de la Victoire—not the only service that the Rothschild family has performed for its co-religionists.

7. Cellar and Chai

IF one were to imagine 21, Rue Laffitte, Paris as a Rothschild army-group headquarters, with Baron Guy, head of de Rothschild Frères, the family bank, with all its ramifications, as commander-in-chief, then Baron Elie is an army commander, with Château Lafite one of his many different divisions in the field, consisting of three brigades: the vineyard; the *chais* and cellars; and the vehicle and machinery park; with André Portet, the *régisseur*, or director, as its major-general commanding.

And André Portet is the very model of a modern major-general.

Most of the great vineyards of the Bordelais, whether in the Médoc, the Graves, or Sauternes, are governed either by a vigneron who has come up the hard way, and been promoted eventually from *maître de chai*, or *chef de culture*, to *régisseur*—to major-general, as it were, from brigadier[1]—or by a man of business who looks after prices, paper-work and administration, leaving a great deal of control over the actual wine-making in the hands of the *maître de chai*. Other distinguished châteaux, especially in the Médoc, are now owned by *négociants*, shippers, who live in Bordeaux, only half-an-hour's drive away, so that they are constantly

---

[1] In the English sense of the word, though the French sense, that of non-commissioned officer, conveys more accurately the class distinction between a *maître de chai* and a *régisseur*.

at the vineyards or the *chais*, giving orders and making decisions, conducting themselves virtually as their own *régisseurs*.

Lafite is different.

André Portet, a biggish, quietly-spoken man in his middle fifties, with a square face and a soldierly bearing, is one of the very few—one of only half-a-dozen perhaps in the whole of deeply traditional wine-growing France—to have been brought into a great vineyard directly at the *régisseur* level because he is a graduate of an agricultural college: the famous Ecole Nationale Supérieure d'Agronomie de Montpelier, which is not only an agricultural college in general but in particular the university of wine-growing and wine-making.

What is also remarkable to find in France, where every region —every village, even—is still deeply jealous, if not actually suspicious and contemptuous, of every other; and where Bordeaux wines are made by Bordelais, burgundy by Burgundians; is that the greatest wine of the Médoc is made not by a Médocain, not even by a Bordelais, but by a Charentais, whose forbears for four or five hundred years—and André Portet himself, until he came to Lafite in 1955, and still by deputy—have grown the thin sharp wine of Cognac and then made brandy out of it: not wine-growers in any sense that the Médoc would understand, but distillers, and on a small scale, selling their product to the great brandy houses.

There is a wind of change in the Bordelais, and it is the noblest vineyards that are being stirred by it. For it is significant that the one other major château in the region where the *régisseur* is not only an agricultural-college graduate but a 'foreigner'—in this case from as far away as the Jura—is Château d'Yquem, the wine of which, officially at any rate, is even more outstanding among the luscious sweet Sauternes than Lafite is among the clarets, for it is listed not simply first among four first growths, as Lafite is, but as the only *Grand Premier Cru*, with the next wines of the district, such fine wines as Coutet and Climens among them, classified as no more than mere *Premiers Crus*.

A stranger, then, to the region, and to the wines of Bordeaux, though not to wine-growing, André Portet was appointed to the directorship of Lafite when the position had to be filled at rather short notice, a dozen years ago, and my guess—which can hardly now be confirmed—is that the choice was something of a Rothschild (or a Baron Elie) hunch.

If so, the personality of the man must have had something to do with it. Now, a dozen years later, he confesses freely that for his first couple of years at Lafite he was, as he puts it, having to ask questions of the *maître de chai* and the *chef de culture* without letting them know that he did not already know the answers—or even that he was asking questions.

Even then, both to such senior subordinates and, earlier, when he was being interviewed by Baron Elie, the quiet authority of the man must have been as impressive as it is now, when there is no mistaking the deference—easy and friendly though it is— shown him by his heads of department: cellar-master, head vigneron, and transport manager.

André Portet is in charge, and is clearly to be seen to be in charge. With his wife, he lives in a comfortable flat above his office in the château's modest south wing, and they take their ease of a summer's evening on the château lawns, under one of the magnolias, or the spreading cedar, as other members of the staff do not.

His eldest son, Bernard, is now himself at Montpelier, eager to follow in father's footsteps—save that there is nowhere, to the minds of either of them, in the same class as Lafite for him to move on to. And André Portet himself, always quietly confident, is now quietly proud: a Charentais, and one of the new breed of professional *agronomes*, he has seen the wine he makes fetch a higher price, every year since he has been here, than any made in the Médoc by *régisseurs* who have been born and spent their lives here, each in his own vineyard. A higher price, probably, than any other recently-vintaged red wine in the world.

So absolute is André Portet's authority at Lafite that he has no deputy. When he goes back to his family home in the Charente for his fortnight's holiday before the vintage, none of his three departmental chiefs is even nominally in charge. There is a conference before he goes away, and the work for the next couple of weeks is agreed upon; were there to be a crisis, he would be telephoned.

All the same, of these three departmental heads that I have already mentioned—*the maître de chai*, the *chef de culture* and the *chef de parc* (which is to say, the vehicle and farm-tractor pool), each answerable direct to the *régisseur*, the *maître de chai* is the senior, or first among equals, his dignity underlined by the fact that at Lafite he, and he alone, holds the key to the *chai*: neither the *régisseur* nor Baron Elie himself holds a duplicate.

Lafite's *maître de chai* is Georges Revelle, born in 1903, who first came to work here when he was only thirteen, son and grandson of workers at Lafite, but the first of his family to hold his present high office, to which he was promoted in 1943 (Plate IX). Georges Revelle, at sixty-four, is slightly built, a little bowed at the shoulders, with stiff grizzled hair, and a stiff, clipped, grizzled moustache. His dark eyes are bright; his worn face has a permanent quizzical shadow of a smile; and he speaks quietly but with animation. He wears a faded blue shirt, tieless, and the shabby suit of a French working-man, and his hands are thick and gnarled, but he is a master of his craft and, alone among such masters,—and there are many distinguished *maîtres de chai*—he is entitled to wear in his lapel the thread of the *Légion d'Honneur*, to which he was appointed in 1959, for his services to wine.

Among his team of fifteen in the *chais* and the *caves* are his son, Robert, born in 1932, who began his training in the cooperage at Lafite and is now concerned with vinification and bottling, and his son-in-law, Henri Biguereau, born in 1925, who takes visitors around and is also in charge of despatch. At the time I write, Henri has only daughters, but Robert has a son of four: there may yet be a fifth generation of Revelles in the service of Lafite.

*   *   *

A *chai* is a shed in which wine is made or stored. Like the sherry *bodegas* of Spain, it is a sort of above-ground cellar. A *cave* is a cellar, proper. Most claret châteaux have only a *chai* or *chais*, which is why the title of the office held by Georges Revelle is *maître de chai*, though Lafite, in fact, has two *chais* and two *caves*.

More than once, and at various times of the year, I have walked through its *chais* and its *caves*, alone or with Georges Revelle, but this is no more (except, perhaps, for the privilege of Georges

Revelle's guidance) than is permitted to any visitor to Lafite, French or foreign, who takes the trouble to ask beforehand. Save only that visitors are not admitted during the actual vintage, when everyone is too busy to be bothered—and this is the one time that there is any bustle of activity in the *chai*. At other times, the cool, dimly-lit, one-storey shed (although above ground, its floor is below ground-level, and its windows are small, and usually shuttered) is as quiet as a church.

Almost two hundred feet long, one of the two biggest in the region (the other being its own next-door twin, to which the new wine will soon be transferred) the *cuvier* or *chai des cuves*—the fermenting shed—holds twenty-four great *cuves*, vats, of Bosnian oak, all of them seventy years old, each bearing its number on an enamel label, and each with a capacity of rather more than three thousand gallons (Plate X).

At vintage time, the wagons with the bunches of grapes back up against the doors and shoot their loads into the *chai*, where they are rotated in cylindrical machines that strip them of their stalks, after which the then broken-skinned grapes, with their juice, are pumped through pipes into the great vats, where the juice will ferment, the skins gradually deepening the colour of the must and, with the pips, providing some of the tannin that will give body and staying-power to the wine. Some tannin comes later from the new wood of the casks.

Until some twenty years ago, the process of *égrappage*—the stripping of the grapes from the stalks—was done by hand: men stood around big tables with latticed tops, over which they gently rubbed the bunches until the grapes separated themselves from the stalks and twigs and fell through to the trays beneath, where they were lightly pressed. This process was revived during the 1964 vintage, because Baron Elie wanted to show it to his English cousin, Lord Rothschild, visiting Lafite for the vintage: Baron Elie has a nostalgic but irrational preference for the old method and admits only grudgingly that the new one is as good. And, of course, infinitely quicker: nowadays, André Portet says it takes less than one-tenth the time it took by hand. Lafite, which has taken the lead in much of the mechanization of vine-tending and wine-handling, has always been cautious in adopting mechanical devices that might prove to be inferior to the natural processes of actual wine-making, and was one of the last of the Médoc vineyards to take to the *égrappage* machine, where it had been the first to mechanize ploughing and spraying.

For ten to twelve days, once the grapes are in the vats, it is temperature that matters: Georges Revelle is constantly taking the temperature of the vats and, with his saccharometer, the sugar content of the must. Each vat has a chart like that of a hospital patient, but with two curves, for as the temperature rises the sugar content must drop, showing that the natural sugar of the grape is being converted into alcohol.

The yeast cells, or ferments, that perform this miracle of turning grape sugar into alcohol, juice into wine, become normally active at about 15°C and die at about 38°C. To make a fine claret, the limits are somewhat narrower: the temperature should not fall below 19°C or rise above 30°C. If it begins to fall too near the lower figure, the vats must be warmed up, which is done by heating a little of the must in a copper boiler and putting it into the first vat, which by some sympathetic process sets off the others. If it approaches the higher figure, the vats must be cooled off, lest the fermentation should stop before all the sugar has been converted. This is done by drawing off the must into another vat, to allow air-cooling, or by coiling pipes round the vats through which cold water is pumped—the milder remedy being tried first.

The must goes into the fermenting vats in the order in which the grapes are gathered, so that one vat may contain only Merlot, another only Cabernet Sauvignon, a third a mixture of both. (Some of the individual vineyards of Lafite grow only one type of vine, some more.)

Fermentation is assisted by aerating the must, which is done by circulating it through pipes—decanting it, as it were—from the big vats to receiving vats and back again, during its first day.

The must is then blended in the proper proportions of the various types of grape by being drawn off into barrels and then back into the fermenting vats: the process takes about fifteen days, and sixty barrels a day are filled and then emptied back into the vats.

When fermentation is complete, the infant wine is drained away to be put into cask. This is the *vin de goutte*, expressed from the skins without any pressure other than the process of fermentation and the weight of skins and pips, the residue of which, the *marc*, is then lightly pressed in wooden presses, and pressed again, to produce a slightly harder *vin de première presse* and a slightly harder still *vin de seconde presse*, richer in tannin and colour than the *vin de goutte*.

André Portet and Georges Revelle taste the fine first wine to decide how much to add of the first pressing to augment its body, colour and tannin. The light wine of a year that has been poor in sunshine, or the gathering of which has been rained on, so that there is water on the skins, may need a fair amount: the potentially 'big' wine of a fine sunny year that culminated in a completely successful vintage may need very little, though some of the first pressing is always added: a year that is too sunny can result in a potentially 'flabby' wine, and also needs *vin de presse* for the sake of its greater firmness of flavour, and backbone of character.

Lafite does not distil an *eau de vie de marc* from this now fairly solid residual cake of pips and skins: none of the Bordeaux vineyards does that I know of, though it is the custom in Burgundy to make this strong, earthy, colourless spirit, as the Italians make *grappa*. Just the sort of thing those coarse-grained Burgundians *would* make—and drink—is the Bordelais view. Here, it is sold to make industrial alcohol. All the *vin de seconde presse*, and what *vin de première presse* is not used at Lafite for adding to the *vin de goutte* is used as a *vin de table* for staff, or for the château's second and third wines.[1]

The wine of Lafite is matured in wood for about two-and-a-half to very nearly three years: bottling, that is, begins in the February or March of the third year after the vintage, and goes on for about six months. Thus, the château began its bottling of the Lafite 1964 in March 1967, and finished it in July (Plate XII).

Where so much is beyond criticism—certainly beyond the criticism of foreigners who do not themselves make wine—this

[1] The Carruades de Château Lafite and the Moulin des Carruades. See pages 117–18.

is the one chapter in the whole process of wine-production at Château Lafite about which I have known Englishmen express their doubts. Bottling is well understood in the English wine trade, and there are firms of bottlers, as well as professional bottlers on the staffs of wine-shipping firms, in London and Bristol and Liverpool and elsewhere, who know more about their craft than is known at many a schloss or clos or château: to a greater extent than many a German or Frenchman who must turn his hand to various tasks in the cellar or the vineyard, they are specialists. Their argument is that a château is geared to the making of wine, not to its bottling; that too often a crisis in the vineyard or a problem presented in *chai* or *cave* is allowed to hold up bottling, which should be as brief and as continuous a process as possible, conducted by men who do nothing else. How, they ask, can a bottle of a fine 1964 claret bottled in February 1967, say, be identical with a bottle of the same wine bottled in July? It will have had five fewer months of drawing tannin from the cask, five more months of the bottle-age that gives softness and mellowness to the wine.

I have put this argument at Lafite to André Portet and Georges Revelle, and their answer is that in a great and, therefore, a long-lived wine, the margin of time at issue becomes proportionately negligible. What matters much more, they say, is how the wine is cellared after it has left the château.

My own opinion is that even the greatest wines nowadays are made to mature more quickly than they used to do, and that the period of as much as five months that is in question has become proportionately greater than once it would have been. Certainly, in 1966, I tasted two bottles of the famous 1953 Lafite, within a few weeks of each other, that had been equally carefully looked after, both in London cellars of the same sort. One was superb; the other, though delicious, was already showing its age, both in colour and in taste, compared with the 1953 Château Margaux against which we were tasting it. I am convinced that the second bottle had been one of the earlier batch at the bottling, and that the result of the extra tannin and shorter period of bottle-age in the first, even as much as ten years after the bottling, was still a greater vigour and youthfulness.

For something like forty years now, the first growths (and some of the other finest wines) of the Médoc have insisted on château-bottling all their own wines: Château Margaux was the last, in 1949, to ship any of its wine in cask, for London-bottling. No doubt the phrase, *mis en bouteille au château*, on the label of an expensive wine carries an especial authority and an incontrovertible authenticity. The American market for fine wines has become very insistent on it, and the American market grows in importance. So the last word is with the château, but I still think that even at the very greatest of them the process of bottling is not yet accorded quite the dignity and importance it deserves.

To be fair, though, I must tell the sequel to my own story of the 1953 Lafite.

I had been so unnerved by its showing evidence of age so early, that before I had taken the time to console myself with the explanation that batches bottled at various times would age at varying rates, and the hope that mine was one of the longer-lived batch, I sent off to Christie's wine sales some magnums I had bought in 1960 when my son was born. I could not now believe that they were going to last until he was twenty or so, in 1980.

When, a year afterwards, I told this story to Mr Ronald Barton, who himself grows fine claret at Léoville-Barton and at Langoa, and whose own 1953 Léoville he thinks is the best wine he has made in forty years of wine-growing, he said, 'You'll regret it'. He admires the wine of Lafite enormously, and he agreed with André Portet and Georges Revelle that the few months of bottle-age involved are not important—that what matters is how the wine is kept.

He went on to make a further point. In his opinion, all fine wines that develop in bottle go through a bad patch—it is like a pretty little girl, he said, who will almost certainly have a spell of spots or of puppy fat, or both, before growing up into a beautiful young woman. I had sold that 1953 Lafite, he said, in its spotty adolescence, and some luckier, or braver, lover than I was would enjoy its maturer charms. 'And in magnums, too...!' he added, shaking his head.

*   *   *

After ten to twelve days in the fermenting vat, the new wine is pumped from vat to cask—to the cask in which it will remain until it is bottled. (Casks vary in the various wine-growing regions of France. The Bordeaux cask is a *barrique* of 225 litres, or 50 gallons, which in England we call a hogshead.) Lafite makes its own casks—out of oak from the 25,000 acre State forest of Tronçais, in the Auvergne, which also provides the casks in which cognac is matured, so that the smell of the cooperage at Lafite comes to André Portet's nostrils as a whiff of home.

Each cask serves one vintage only. That is to say that from the fermenting vat the new wine goes into a brand-new cask, and stays in that cask (or, as it is racked, as will be explained later, in one of the same batch) for the two-and-a-half or three years that it matures in wood until it is bottled, though the cask is moved from *chai* to cellar, and from one cellar to another during this period. When the wine is bottled, the cask is sold: it cannot be used again for Lafite.

The *chai de la première année* adjoins the *chai des cuves*, and is also some couple of hundred feet long, or very nearly. The wine from the twenty-four vats is pumped into as many as are needed of the thousand brand-new and, to romantics, disappointingly light-coloured oak barrels that have been manhandled into the *chai*, bungholes uppermost, which are then stoppered simply, for this first year, by laying a sort of heavy glass globe on the hole. This is the practice throughout the region: M. Alexis Lichine, of Château Lascombes, tells of taking an American woman visitor to Château Latour who observed how cute it must look when they were all lit up. (At Lafite in 1961, at the dinner given by Baron Elie and the Baroness to the guests at the wedding, the previous day, of the daughter of Baron Philippe de Rothschild, of Château Mouton, lighted candles were in fact placed *on* the glass bungs.)

A scribble of chalk on each cask serves to show which vat it has been filled from. Every other day for a year one of Georges Revelle's men goes round them all, peering into each bunghole to see how much of the new wine has evaporated through the new wood, and making good the loss, always filling up each cask with wine from the vat that it was originally filled from. This is the *ouillage*—the same word as the English 'ullage', which we use in the opposite sense, in that we speak of a cask or a bottle that shows a loss by evaporation as being 'ullaged'.

Four times in that first year the wine is 'racked'. During these early months of its life, it drops various solid impurities to the bottom of the cask, and it must be drawn off, from one cask to another, a sort of decanting called here the *soutirage*, leaving the impurities behind, besides refreshing itself in the process with the oxygen from the air that helps it to mature.

Towards the end of this first year, after four such rackings, those impurities that are still left in the wine are too light to fall to the bottom of the cask under their own weight, and the wine must be 'fined', or clarified. This is the process of *collage*, for which various patented chemical preparations exist, but effected here, where all is kept as natural and as traditional as is consistent with efficiency, by white of egg: for each cask, the whites of six to eight eggs are whisked with a bundle of twigs in a small wooden bowl called a *bontemps*, mixed with wine, and poured into the cask, where the mixture is stirred with a metal instrument in figures of eight for about ten minutes, then gradually sinking to the bottom, carrying with it the last impurities (Plate XI).

The wooden bowl, the *bontemps*, gives its name to the confraternity of owners, shippers and those who, like myself, are simply amateurs of Bordeaux wines, known as the Commanderie du Bontemps de Médoc et des Graves: unlike the Jurade of St Emilion, it has no long, unbroken history as a trade guild, but was created in 1950 as a promotional device and as an agreeable excuse for dressing up in medieval robes, and enjoying good dinners. The Commanderie holds its major investitures each June, at a different château every year, at the same time as the Fête de la Fleur celebrates the flowering of the vine. (There are other, smaller, investitures from time to time.) The velvet robes of the order are claret-coloured, of course, as is the round, cup-shaped cap, in which a ruching of white silk symbolizes the white of egg frothing in the *bontemps*.

Dates have to be fixed well ahead: sometimes the *fête* comes before the *fleur*, but the châteaux wear their flags—some, such as Langoa-Barton and Angludet their Union flags; Château Palmer, in joint and international ownership, the Union flag and both the French and the Dutch tricolours, and Château Rausan-Ségla not only the Union flag but also the house flag of John Holt and Company of Liverpool, to which it belongs—and the festivities, the luncheon and the speeches go on virtually all day. The French make and eat longer and heavier luncheons than the English, and they make and listen to longer and heavier after-luncheon speeches.

Each year, for the *collage* at Lafite, the whites of something like six or seven thousand eggs are used. The yolks go to the workers' families, and there is a brief, liverish season of the richest omelettes and crèmes. It would be agreeable to be able to record here some traditional Bordelais recipes based on the yolks of eggs but there seems, alas, to be none. I had hoped, for instance, for the *crème bacchique* of Tante Marie's famous cookery book, which is a custard made of yolks of egg and Sauternes. They may make it in the Sauternais, but I have never come across it in the Médoc when I have been there at the appropriate time: only scrambled eggs as an *hors d'oeuvre* course; heavy omelettes; and grumbles about how liverish it all is.

Meanwhile, the whites are doing their work in the casks, which have now been moved to the *cave de seconde année*, each cask turned over a few degrees so that the bunghole, now stoppered with wood, is in contact with the wine, being kept moist so that it will not shrink in drying, and thus let in the air. The fining of white of egg falls slowly through the wine, like a veil, carrying with it the fine solid matter into a sediment at the bottom of the cask that can sometimes become as much as four or five inches deep.

Three times in its second year of life, and a fourth time in its third year—its last year in wood—the wine is racked again, leaving its lees behind. At the beginning of its third year it has been moved to the *cave de troisième année*, its last resting place before being pumped through gleaming glass pipes to the bottling plant.

Lafite is possibly unique among the châteaux of the Médoc in using *caves*, not *chais*, for these last two years of maturing in wood. They are rather cooler even than the *chai* of the *cuves* and of the first year, and André Portet believes that this means a slightly slower and steadier maturing, and a consequently longer life for the wine: it was only recently, under his régime, that a second *cave* was tunnelled under the courtyard, making it possible for each vintage to spend two years in cellar after one in shed, instead of two in shed and one in cellar.

Lafite tends each year to be lighter in tannin than its peers, particularly than the stubborn Latour, and while there is advantage in a wine's becoming ready to drink in a reasonably short time, nevertheless if it comes on too quickly it will not have had time to develop its full quality and style—its personality, so to speak. A youngster may well have charm, but it is only when he reaches full manhood that he develops character. Lafite is an eager as well as an elegant wine, and having been made so in the vineyard and the vat, it is treated in the cellars rather as a wise schoolmaster will handle a quick, clever boy—taking him through his schooling just that shade more deliberately, lest he become superficial.

Whipping up whites of egg in a *bontemps* with a bunch of twigs, preparatory
to fining the wine in the barrels

PLATE XI

'Mis en bouteilles au château'

PLATE XII

The 'library' with its collection of old wines

PLATE XIII

The vigneron's year begins in November with the pruning of the vines
(Inset—close-up of pruning)

PLATE XIV

8. Vineyard and Vine

WHEN I first tasted the 1966 Lafite, drawn by pipette from a cask in the *chai de la première année*, I was in the company not only of André Portet, the *régisseur*, and Georges Revelle, the *maître de chai*, but also of André Lavanceau, who had been *chef de culture* at Lafite from 1945 until this wine had been vintaged, a few months before, when he had retired, on the eve of his seventieth birthday. He beamed with pride at our compliments on what we knew already was going to be a majestic Lafite— full, yet delicate; soft, yet with staying-power; and with all the legendary fragrance of Lafite. The best wines that had been made at Lafite in his time, he said, were that of his first year as *chef de culture*, and that of his last, and he told me again the story that nobody at Lafite will tire of telling until the next great stroke of wine-grower's luck—or of wine-grower's genius: how in 1966, after the first day's picking, he and the *régisseur* decided to telephone Baron Elie in Paris, and urge him to call a halt, and postpone the rest, which was virtually the whole, of the vintage until a week later than every other château in the Médoc: how foolish or how rash everyone in Bordeaux and Pauillac had said they were, and how wise they had proved to be.

The last word on the date to pick, like the last word on everything at Lafite, is Baron Elie's, but the advice he acts upon is that of the *régisseur* and the *chef de culture*, who is responsible for the grapes until the very moment that they are taken to the *chai des cuves*. From about the middle of September onwards, André Portet and his *chef de culture*—André Lavanceau then, and now Michel Picabea, once his pupil—are in the vineyards daily, inspecting and fingering and tasting the grapes, cocking their eyes as much at the skies as at the weather reports, trusting as much to their own experience and judgment as to the laboratory's analyses of the sugar-content and the acidity of the grapes.

They balance the certainty of a sound vintage now, when the grapes are ripe enough—neighbouring châteaux are already picking or about to pick, and the weather seems settled for the fortnight or so that the vintage will last—against the chance of a better vintage still, if everything is put off, with the grapes having become that much riper, with more sugar, which means more alcohol, with more colour in the skins, and less acidity, but with the attendant risk of rain in the meantime, and the consequence of anything from simply a poorer, lighter, vintage because of rain-water on the grape-skins, and a washing-away of the yeasts that bring about fermentation, to the utter ruin that can befall if violently heavy and continuous autumn rainstorms—or even hail—shatter the vines.

Fortune favours the brave.

MM. Portet and Lavanceau have always inclined to pick late rather than early, and although many châteaux in the Médoc also now tend to pick later than they used to do, Lafite often picks latest of all. In 1967, for instance, Lafite began to pick five days later than Mouton, the next vineyard, and went on for a full week longer. And this in spite of the fact that there is much more Merlot at Lafite than at Mouton, and the Merlot ripens earlier than the Cabernet Sauvignon and Cabernet Franc. But for years past the sun has been, as André Portet puts it, 'with Lafite', and year after year the wine has benefited by the greater softness and suppleness, and the lower acidity, that the extra ripeness brings—as well as the quicker maturing of the wine, which is of economic importance to shippers and wine-merchants and restaurateurs, who need thus tie up their capital for a shorter time than the greatest and most expensive wines used to take to become ready to drink, and which in turn makes Lafite all the more sought after, among the greatest clarets.

There have been disappointments, of course. Not through the policy of late picking, unless one regards the vintage of 1964 as such a disappointment, and for this reason. Fine wine was made that year, but the last days of the vintage were lost through a decision by Baron Elie to hold up things up for a day or so longer so that his English kinsman, Lord Rothschild, could see a Lafite vintage. It rained.

But the major disappointments have been due to the Merlot's falling a prey to *coulure*, the disease of 'floral abortion', which means that the flower falls away from the vine without forming fruit. It was because of this that the 1947 and 1957 Lafite, though sound wines, were hard, lacking the finesse, the softness and the fragrance that the Merlot gives—good enough to bear the Lafite label, but not typical Lafite. But there has been nothing for a generation now like that disastrous decade of 1927–1936, five vintages of which—those of 1927, 1930, 1932, 1935 and 1936— were not labelled as Lafite at all, but *déclassé*, by a decision of the château itself, because of the damage done by continuous rain, to being 'Pauillac' simply.

Of the wines he has made himself, during his quarter of a century as *maître de chai*, Georges Revelle agrees with André Lavanceau about the 1945, and brackets that and the 1953 together as those he is proudest of—the 1945 harder to begin with, but now drinking splendidly as, in his opinion, the 1953 is, in 1967.[1] It may be, he says, that there will in future be fewer such hard wines as the 1945—except, of course, through a failure of the Merlot, as in 1957. For it is in these last couple of decades that the practice has developed of late picking, which means, as I have said, quicker maturing. Even more positively, Georges Revelle says that he does not expect to see again such an extremely slow-doer as the 1926 Lafite, which is only now showing its real charm.

*   *   *

[1] But see page 95.

With the laurels of that historic 1966 decision still green upon his brow, André Lavanceau—big, hearty and erect at seventy—now lives in happy retirement at Le Pouyalet, the village that lies almost at the gates of Lafite, with his own garden and even his own little vineyard. Geographically, at any rate, his seventy years have not taken him very far, for he was born in one of the workers' cottages at Lafite, where his father, like Georges Revelle's, was a vigneron, as his grandfather and his great-grandfather were before him: there were Lavanceaux at Lafite before there were Rothschilds. (A younger brother, now in his middle sixties, holds a similarly dignified position at another notable establishment of the district—he is head-waiter at that admirable Bordeaux restaurant, the Château Trompette.)

And I suppose it is a sign of the times that although old André Lavanceau is immensely proud of this family record, as he is of the wine of Lafite, which he simply knows, without question, that you, to whom he is talking, also know, also without question, to be the greatest wine in the world, and as he is of having worked for the Rothschilds ('they gave us social security before France did: sick pay, doctor's bills, chemist's prescriptions, everything . . .')—in spite of all this; in spite even of that vast cedar there on the lawn having been planted a century ago, as a sapling, by a Lavanceau; he is not at all disappointed, he says, that his only son works, not at Lafite, but at the Shell refinery in Pauillac, the gleaming metal tanks of which you can see from the château terrace. There is more future in it for him, he says: the world is different now.

But Lafite is not. André Lavanceau began work there in 1908, when he was a boy of eleven, and in sixty years, although he has seen horses (and the oxen that took their place during two world wars) give way to machines, and the space between the rows of vines increased from eighty centimetres to a metre, to make room for them, there seem to have been few other major changes (Plate XV).

Nobody at Lafite imagines that there can be any possible changes in the foreseeable future. At Château Latour, for instance, they have special new metal fermenting vats, with outer and inner skins between which one can force hot or cold water to correct the temperature of fermentation, but although everybody at Lafite respects Latour they have no wish at all to go and do likewise: it simply would not be Lafite. It is rather like the attitude of the traditionalist Madame Bollinger, in Champagne, to the enterprising Comte Robert de Vogüé at Moet and Chandon.

*   *   *

Yvan Harribey, the *chef de parc* at Lafite, is in his late forties. Like his two fellow department-heads, André Lavanceau and Georges Revelle, he comes of a family long connected with Lafite: his father was a carter there, and died almost literally in harness; his mother's father worked there, and so did his wife's grandfather.

He has eleven men under him—the estate's painters, electricians and mason, as well as the drivers—and four tractors for the vineyards; two for road work; and a truck. He thinks that perhaps he could do with one more tractor, to feel really well-equipped, but that is all: when I asked him if he could foresee any further mechanization of wine-growing or wine-making, even this mechanically-minded man, who would share in any gain in importance by the machines, was surprised at such a suggestion, and when I asked about mechanical picking, he was more than surprised; he was shocked, as André Portet was.

That sort of thing might be all very well for hops: it might even come to it for the *vins courants* of the Midi, though he had never heard tell of such, even there. But a fine wine depended on getting the grapes to the *cuves* in perfect condition, and with no damage to the bloom on their skins, in which are the natural yeasts that will bring about fermentation. How could one ensure that with machines?

Mind you, says André Lavanceau, there have been slight changes in the *encèpagement*: the Malbec grape never does so well in the gravel and sand of the Lafite vineyards as it does in the chalk of St Emilion, and it has gone out of production. The Merlot, always delicate, but important to the château's style, does better now that it is better understood and cared for—there is more of it here than at the other first-growth châteaux, though even so it is only a minor constituent of the *encèpagement* of Lafite.

Then, too, there has been some small extension of the area under vines. When André Lavanceau first began work here there were seventy-five hectares, which dwindled to fifty in the 1930s, when vintages were bad, and so were the stock markets, so that men who had once been rich were in no state to buy wines that had once been good. The great vintage of 1945 reminded the wine-drinking world of the splendours of claret and, as it promised to be a long-lived wine, of how good an investment it was. There were new markets in which to sell it, as well as old fortunes that had been restored, and replanting began. Now there are eighty hectares under vines at Lafite—just a very few more than when the eleven-year-old André Lavanceau began his life's work.

Apart from that, and apart from the fact that he used to see Rothschilds come to Lafite by Rothschild yacht to Pauillac and then by carriage, where now it is by Rothschild aeroplane and then by motor-car, little has changed.

*   *   *

Little, indeed, does change in a major vineyard, where wine is made seriously, and the natural processes of growth are not interfered with, but merely helped along.

The vigneron's year begins in November (Plate XIV), after the excitements of the *vendange* are over, with the *taille*, or pruning, of the vines, cutting away half-a-dozen branches from each, to leave two or, at most, three. These, in February and March, after old stakes and wires have been renewed, will be trained along the wire a couple of dozen inches from the ground, in the traditional *pliage* of the Gironde, bending up a little and then down again, in a graceful flat curve, so that the sap does not race straight to the end of the branch, as André Lavanceau explained it to me (he called it, 'the blood'), but has time to nourish flower, leaf and fruit on the way.

Meanwhile, there has been the *fumage*—the manuring of the vines with cow-dung for, although the vine flourishes in poor soil, what it takes out of it must be put back. And the soil is poor, indeed, in those parts of Lafite where the vine flourishes: during the war, they tried potatoes and maize there with no success. 'If we didn't grow grapes', says André Portet, 'it would have to be lucerne.' And it is lucerne that they grow in those fields where old vines have been uprooted, for the five years before new ones are planted.

March is a treacherous month, its saints known as *les geleurs de vignes*—freezers of the vines—and April can be cruel, too: the vignerons do not rub their hands with relief until St Urbain's day, as late as May 25, has passed without frost damage. All being well, though, April and May are the months when old vines and seedy ones are pulled up, and new ones planted—about five per cent, 35,000 or so, of the total number of vines at Lafite are pulled up and replaced every year. Generally speaking, a vine bears after five years and makes respectable wine after seven; after thirty years or so it is making better wine but less of it; and its useful life is over, as a rule, by the time it is fifty, though there are vines at Lafite that date back to 1896, kept more as curiosities than as useful members of the community of vines: they are hard by the château, and are something to show off and talk about.

Now comes the first of the year's four ploughings. Twice, in May and in July, the soil is loosened (*déchaussage*) by the tractor-drawn plough, and drawn away by a vigneron with a hoe (*tirage les cavaillons*) from the roots of the vine, so as to clear away grass and weeds, and aerate the soil. Twice, in June and in August, alternately with the other ploughings, the plough loosens the soil and the vigneron with his hoe banks it back again over the roots (*boutage*).

The vine's first tender shoots appear in May: they are pruned vigorously, and now begins the spraying against mildew, oïdium, and the various insects that prey upon the vine—spraying with sulphur, copper sulphate, lime, D.D.T. and the various proprietary insecticides that advertise themselves on the gable-ends of French wine-growing villages as aperitifs do elsewhere, or the table waters that, so disconcertingly to the touring Englishman, go 'Psch . . . itt!'

In small vineyards, even in the Médoc, you may still see the vignoron doing it all by hand, as I have seen them at Duhart-Milon, which is immediately next to Château Lafite, to which it now belongs, the men with tanks on their backs and sprays in their hands; at Lafite the tractor-drawn machine, driven by one man, sprays six rows at a time. (The smallest vineyards of all make do with journeymen sprayers, who do the rounds of the peasant-proprietors with their van and their apparatus.)

The greatest vineyard plague of all, the phylloxera, which devastated the vineyards of Europe almost a century ago, is now unknown, except as the villain of a bogey-tale: it has been eradicated, at Lafite as throughout France, and in France as throughout Europe, by grafting the European *vitis vinifera* on to American *vitis labrusca* roots, which are resistant to the root louse that found the European vines such easy victims.

The sprayings continue now until the vintage: it is the copper-sulphate spray, against the mildew, that turns the vine-leaves the hard, metallic bluish-green so familiar to those of us who drive through France in high summer to the sunshine of the south.

It is high summer now at Lafite, too. The flower of the vine came in early June, smaller than a mignonette, and with no scent. The châteaux beflag themselves for the Fête de la Fleur. The red and pink roses that the claret-growers plant where the ends of the rows of vines meet the road are in full bloom—this is a new custom in the Bordelais, and a pretty one;—Lafite observes it in the vineyard that lies opposite the château on the Pauillac–St Estèphe road, though there are some châteaux that refuse to follow suit: Baron Philippe de Rothschild at Mouton says that roses 'detract from the dignity of the vine'.

The gravel crunches on the drives of the grandest châteaux (especially at Mouton, with its museum, and at Lascombes, with its annual exhibition of pictures, *La Vigne et le Vin*), as the cars drive up with their sightseers—Volkswagens and Mini-Minors, and Americans, hung with cameras, in hired cars, but more French than foreigners, for this is on the road to nowhere very much, and a beaten track mainly for those who care about wine, to whom the name of the châteaux strung along the *chemin départemental* D2—Cantemerle and Margaux, Beychevelle and Mouton, Latour and Lafite—sound like trumpets or, to a Frenchman, like Napoleon's calling the roll of his marshals.

It is hot now, hot and tiring. Or so it is usually, though the weather of the Médoc can be as changeable as England's. I write

this very paragraph in July, at Lafite, looking up from my table
to see, through the window, a grey windless sky hanging vertical
curtains of grey rain over the grey stone of the terrace balustrade,
the red roses and the distant heavy green curves of chestnut
trees. In its coolness, as in its colour, nothing could seem more
English.

As often as not, though, from June to September, the air
between Gironde and Atlantic, between broad river and broad
ocean, is humid and heavy. There is haze and there is cloud,
which is just as well, they tell you in the vineyards, because when
the sun does shine, it shines hard in these parts, and although the
grapes need sun now, too much or too hot sunshine and they
could become *grillés*: grapes have been known to burn on the
vines in a really hot summer, and the vintage spoiled.

Even a summer not hot enough for that can still be hot enough
to make too much sugar in the grapes, skins too thick and pips
too coarse, and result in a heavy or a flabby wine, or one that is
going to be difficult to ferment. Nor does French law permit,
in the Médoc, any watering whatsoever, at any time of the year,
of vines or of vineyards, whether by sprays or by irrigation
ditches. This is yet another of the restrictions intended to maintain quality even at the expense of quantity. 'It would be the
same as putting water in the milk,' said André Portet.

A vigneron with a great knife like a Mexican *machete*—his
father used a sickle—is making the *écimage*, trimming the random
shoots, as he will three times in all before the end of July, while
his colleagues spray again, and his wife or his daughter adjusts
the uppermost shoots between the upper of the two rows of
wire, which is a double one. This double wire is a Lafite innova-
tion, introduced in 1954, and makes it easy to keep the tendrils
of the vine trim in this process of *palissage*.

From the flowering to the *vendange*, if all goes well, will be one
hundred and twenty days: it is safer, perhaps, to count from the
veraison, somewhere between July 20 and the end of the month,
when the grapes turn from green to red, and it will be two months
to their gathering.

From then on, there is little to do in the vineyards—little that
can be done. The grapes are swelling now, their skins thinning:

they must be left alone, lest they are *blessés*, wounded. The vineyard workers take their eighteen to twenty-four days' holiday,
though few of them go away, except for day trips to relatives:
whatever the new-fangled restless habits of Parisians and the
townsfolk of Bordeaux, the French countryman is still a stay-
at-home. He tends his garden, or goes out fishing. The more
adventurous—or those of them with motor-cars—spend the day
on the beach at Soulac, or Verdon, or cross by the ferry to the
brand spanking new resort of Royan. André Portet goes to his
native Charente for a fortnight, to see his relatives, and Georges
Revelle and his team prepare the *chais* and the *caves*, the *cuves* and
the *barriques*, for the vintage.

This is the climax of the year in the Bordelais. In Bordeaux itself, the shop windows in the Cours de l'Intendance and the Rue
Sainte-Catherine deck themselves with plastic grapes that are
larger than life, and vine-leaves all too artistically autumnal.
Every village in the Médoc reeks of the new must. Along the
river-front at Pauillac rumble trailers bearing heavily stained tubs
of grapes bound for the local co-operative, most of them drawn
nowadays by tractors, a few by pairs of horses, and one or two
still, to the traditionalist's delight, by mules.

At Lafite, vineyard after vineyard comes to life with a gossip-
ing crew of women and youngsters—boys and girls—bending
and straightening, bending and straightening at the heavy clusters. It is only now and again, when the chattering as of starlings
drops for a while, that you can hear what might be taken instead
for grasshoppers—the snip, snap, snip of the secateurs at the
stems.

These are the *coupeurs*, and to every four rows of vines, each
with its four or half-a-dozen *coupeurs*, is a heftier *porteur*, a man
with a shaped *hotte* on his back. The pickers fill each their little
wooden *paniers*, or trugs, and empty them into the *hottes*, and
each *porteur* climbs a little portable ladder to shoot the contents
of his *hottes*, with a neat twist, over his shoulder, into one of the
douils on the trailer. Some of the trailers at Lafite are drawn by
tractors, some by the spider-like machines called *enjambeurs*,
'striders', so built as to straddle the vines and take sprays or
ploughs between them, according to season. Each trailer holds

two or three *douils*, each of which holds 350–400 litres of grapes: a good cutter fills one *douil* in an eight-hour day.

When the weather is good for the vintage of Lafite, the sky is a great unbroken sweep of blue, with a hot hint of haze in the east, over the Gironde, and of red and brown and gold in the great, full-breasted trees, still heavy with leaf, that surround the château itself—though the pickers may often be in a vineyard from which the château is out of sight, and from which the vines stretch to the next rise in the ground, as far as the eye can see.

The vine leaves, too, are turning to red and gold—some more, some less—and the bunches of grapes are blue and bloomy, those of the Cabernet Sauvignon dense and tight, the Merlot with rather bigger berries, in longer and looser clusters.

Each year, the various vineyards of Lafite are picked in much the same order, for they ripen almost invariably according to their exposure to the sun. Almost always, unless there has been disease, those planted with Merlot, or mostly with Merlot, ripen the earliest; then the Cabernet Sauvignon; then the Cabernet Franc. First of all, though, they pick the youngest vines—those that go into the Carruades de Château Lafite, as will be explained later—and sometimes these may still be green when the picking begins.

A very few, still, of the oldest women in the vineyards wear the *quichenotte*—the old-fashioned cotton or linen poke-bonnet, shading much of the face, the name of which is said to derive from 'kiss-not', and to date from the days when the English ruled in Aquitaine. But chiefly there are head-scarves and little linen caps, pinafores and print dresses, to fleck the vineyards with colour. The men wear cloth caps, or berets, or nothing on their heads at all, but many of them have a fag-end dangling from the corner of the mouth, just as most of the younger pickers munch at a cluster of grapes from time to time when the weather is hot. Nobody seeks to muzzle the ox that treads the corn.

The strongest points of colour in the vineyard are the metal *hottes*, which by Médoc tradition (unless they are left unpainted altogether) are painted either green or the deep, spicy, brownish red of paprika. 'But the green isn't really pretty,' says André Portet, so here all the *hottes* are red—exactly the same colour that is so time-honoured as that in which the doors and shutters of *chai* and *cuvier* and the worker's dwellings must be painted that when the Baroness proposed to have them repainted white there was shocked and by no means silent disapproval, and she had to be content with the doors to the offices and the *régisseur's* flat.

Elsewhere in the region—all over wine-growing Europe, in fact—there are students in the vineyards, both French and foreign and, especially in the Médoc, as in Germany, there are itinerant Spanish workers, quick and efficient at the picking, careful with their money and frugal with their food, which they insist on cooking for themselves, and quick to quarrel, which disconcerts the dour French peasants.

Lafite, though, has no dormitory accommodation for such wanderers, and relies entirely on the wives and the adolescent children of the resident vineyard workers and cellarmen, re-inforced by folk from Pauillac and the little villages near by— Mousset and Milon, Loubeyres and Le Payoulet—the families of which have been picking at Lafite every year for generations past.

Some of these are the wives of men who work at the Shell refineries or in this or that local garage—women who do not go out to work during the rest of the year. Some of the men are them-selves small proprietors, whose grapes go to the local co-opera-tives, and their sons. Some come in their own little cars, or on mopeds or bicycles, but most are collected every morning by a hired motor-coach that does an early round of the villages in time for its load to be up at Lafite when the bell rings at half-past eight for the day's work to begin.

The workers are engaged for the whole period of the vintage, so that if a day is lost by rain they are still paid for it, and the pay is for the whole day that a worker is on hand, whether or not every hour can be worked: I have seen vintagers very happily idling away the first two hours of a sunny October day because there had been a particularly heavy dew in the night, and the orders were not to pick until 10 o'clock, lest the grapes went to the vat with too much water on their skins.

There will be about fifteen working days, and for each of them the pay is 18 francs for *coupeurs*, 19 francs for *porteurs*—say, 30s. and

32/6*d*. a day, or £22–£23 or so for the vintage, which is a tidy sum when one considers that all meals are provided—even breakfast—and one litre a day of rough wine (not Lafite!) for the women, two for the men.

The meals are hot, cooked by a brigade of the older resident wives—women built to the scale of the vast kitchen and its great ranges, which are used only for the period of the *vendange*. Two-tiered metal containers of different sizes, with handles—for families of four, of three, of two, and for single workers—each contain a plate of the thin, flavoury, *soupe de vendange*, in which float slices of bread, as well as a hot meat dish, usually some sort of a stew with vegetables. At lunch-time, which lasts from 12.30 till 2, the *vendangeurs* take the containers home, or into a vineyard, or up into a big bare refectory; at 6 every evening they take a similar container home, together with the next morning's cold but substantial breakfast—the principle being that if a woman is working at the *vendange* she must be spared the Frenchwoman's usual task of cooking all day at home.

In the same way, there is a *garderie*—a rough-and-ready nursery—in which children between three and fourteen, whose mothers are in the vineyards, are looked after and fed. Wives of resident staff are expected to take part in the vintage: if their children are over three years old, and they opt out of vintage work, then they do not share in the vintage meals, but if their children are under three they are fed without having to work.

The food is wholesome—the vegetables come from the Lafite kitchen garden—and varied. This is the week's menu that was repeated over the two-and-a-half weeks of the 1967 vintage:

	Breakfast	Lunch	Dinner
Monday	Pâte	Soup Pot au Feu	Soup Pork Cutlets
Tuesday	Sardines	Soup Veal Stew	Soup Hot Sausage & White Beans
Wednesday	Cheese	Soup Roast Pork Mashed Potatoes	Soup Mutton Stew

	Breakfast	Lunch	Dinner
Thursday	Pâté	Soup Hot Sausage & White Beans	Soup Entrecôte
Friday	Cheese	Soup Pot au Feu	Soup Salt Cod
Saturday	Sausage	Soup Beef stewed in Wine	Soup Pork Cutlets
Sunday	Sardines	Soup Veal Cutlets and Peas	Soup Entrecôte

—and there was a helping of apple turnover as well with the Sunday lunch.

I can vouch both for the wholesomeness of the diet, for I took most of these meals myself, with no special favours from the château (save that I drank Lafite with my luncheon and my dinner, where the *vendangeurs* drank *ordinaire*), and also for its heartiness. I have seldom put away so much animal protein in one day as on the Monday on which I had pot au feu at midday and, for my high tea, so to speak, the biggest pork cutlet I have ever seen, grilled over the trunks and branches of old vines, and just deliciously touched with the tang of wood-smoke.

* * *

The men who grow Lafite grow the sort of wine that they themselves like. If they are reluctant to appraise the other first growths, and the wine of their nearest neighbour and closest rival, Mouton, it is not, I think, because of any lack of magnanimity towards their noblest competitors, but quite the reverse—they respect the care and the skill that go into Latour and Haut Brion, Margaux and Mouton, but the styles are all different, between all of them, and between each of them and Lafite, and the differences are such that although—as will be seen later—they can enjoy wines quite unlike their own, they seem unable (or unwilling) to appraise them.

Mouton, in particular, although it marches—and, indeed, at

two points, as we have seen, actually interlocks with Lafite—is notably different in the style of its wine. Partly, this is because of natural differences in the lie of the land and its nature. Mouton's vineyards, on the whole, lie a little flatter than the slightly more undulating slopes of Lafite and, therefore, take the sun differently.

Every wine-grower in the Médoc to whom I have talked about it is sure that even if the *encèpagement* were precisely the same at Mouton and at Lafite the wines would still be different. Mr Ronald Barton, for instance, whose own two wines, Léoville and Langoa, from neighbouring properties, differ markedly, suggests that there may well be slight differences in deep subsoil between the two properties, and in the way the vineyards drain.

But all these differences between Mouton and Lafite are intensified by the great difference in *encèpagement*. At Mouton, Cabernet Sauvignon accounts for no less than 90 per cent of the total, Cabernet Franc for as little as five per cent and Merlot for a mere three or four per cent. (There is a trace—one or two per cent—of Petit Verdot, as there is at Lafite, though there it is even less.)

At Lafite, it will be remembered, the proportion is only two-thirds Cabernet Sauvignon, and one-sixth each of Cabernet Franc and Merlot—about five times as much Merlot as at Mouton, and only two-thirds as much Cabernet Sauvignon.

It is the Cabernet Sauvignon that provides—as well as the much desired regularity in production and resistance to disease—the tannin that gives hardness and staying-power to a wine. The Cabernet Franc gives sugar and, therefore, alcohol. The Merlot, thin-skinned and difficult to rear, gives finesse, fragrance, fruitiness and softness.

This is why Mouton is a bigger, fuller, harder wine than Lafite, —'heavy, full and almost fleshy', is the comment on it in M. Alexis Lichine's *Encyclopaedia of Wines and Spirits*, 'with a special taste that natives of Bordeaux refer to as a *goût de capsule* or "taste of the capsule" ' [which is of lead foil] 'from its distinctive, hard and almost metallic flavour. The high percentages of Cabernet Sauvignon grapes used make it very slow to mature and very full-bodied.'

In Lafite, on the other hand, the high proportion of Merlot

gives what M. Lichine describes as 'great finesse and particular softness', going on to say of it that it 'tends to be firm yet delicate and supple, with an eventual lightness developed in age. Lesser vintages are still excellent wines, lighter than those of great years, but always showing breed, fragrance, and depth of flavour.'

Some claret-lovers prefer Mouton, some Lafite. Some, of course, are so dedicated to their own choice that they cannot abide the other: I have heard a devoted admirer of Lafite say, 'I don't like Mouton, because I don't like burgundy'. But most of us can drink either of them with pleasure—though I cannot imagine anyone liking them equally when each is at its most typical.

Anyway, André Portet and Georges Revelle and the others at Lafite, not having a taste for these other great wines, are not to be drawn about them, lest they should seem ungenerously to disparage. When they are asked what claret they would drink if they did not drink Lafite they prefer to discuss the lesser growths, about one of which indeed Lafite shows virtual unanimity.

Admittedly, there was a minority report from M. Guy Schÿler, who acts as host at Lafite for Baron Elie, and who also has a Bordeaux wine-shipping business of his own. After a compliment to Château Margaux, (which he is not alone in finding to be the first growth nearest in style to Lafite), he nominated Château Gruaud-Larose, but both André Portet and Georges Revelle, although they nodded their understanding of this, added that whereas they found Gruaud-Larose of a good year pleasing in the mouth, they considered that it usually falls a little flat at the finish.

What they both agreed upon was Château Cos d'Estournel and so, later, did André Lavanceau, the head vine-dresser, and Baron Elie himself, when I asked him the same question in Paris.

So four out of five had chosen, as their favourite claret after Lafite itself, a wine that is very different in style—big, hard, full and rich: a fine claret, and long-lasting in bottle, but with nothing like Lafite's suppleness and grace. It may be, of course, that it was this very contrast that interested and attracted them. As well as that, they spoke admiringly, as fellow-craftsmen, of the care and skill with which the wine of Cos d'Estournel is made.

On two sides the trim rows of vines come right up to the château and its buildings.
The distance between the rows has been increased from 80 to 100 centimetres to
make room for modern machinery

PLATE XV

View of Château Lafite on a mid-nineteenth-century Bordeaux earthenware plate, one of a series of plates bearing views of châteaux of the Médoc

Commemorative goblet engraved by Honoria Marsh for the centenary of the Rothschild purchase of Château Lafite

PLATE XVI

Château Cos d'Estournel is Lafite's immediate neighbour to the north: you can see the fantastic little Chinese pagodas on its walls—a bit of nineteenth-century French fantasy—over the trees from the Lafite vineyards.

Mouton is no farther away on the other side, and just as at Lafite they do not make Mouton their second choice, neither does Baron Philippe at Mouton make Lafite his. Again, it came as something of a surprise when he told me that when he dines in a restaurant (as it would be absurd to call for Mouton, which he drinks at its best at home), he always looks first to see if they have a Château Cantemerle of a good year—a light, delicate claret, fast-maturing, that is about as different in style from Mouton as a fine claret can be.

It seemed to me that just as the growers of Lafite had done, Baron Philippe had turned instinctively, for the sake of interest and contrast, to a wine that he respected but that was very unlike his own in character. And it did cross my mind that if the men who make the light, delicate Lafite had made the strapping Cos d'Estournel their second choice, and the man behind the strapping Mouton had opted for a light, delicate Cantemerle, then they might just as well have selected each other. But no doubt the traditional rivalry between these two great wines (which long antedates the Rothschild régime at either) is just a little too deeply felt for that.

It will be interesting to see what André Portet, as *régisseur*, makes of Duhart-Milon, the fourth-growth château immediately adjacent to Lafite on the west, which the Rothschilds bought in 1962, when the *encépagement* was quite different from that of Lafite, but which, through its new *chef de culture*, appointed from the Lafite staff, is being brought into line with its nobler neighbour. 'Ah,' said André Lavanceau, 'if only Baron Elie had bought Cos d'Estournel!' And then laughed at the thought of M. Ginestet's even thinking of selling it, for Cos d'Estournel belongs to the owner of Château Margaux.

Here is the place, perhaps, to mention Carruades de Château Lafite, which is a sort of younger brother of Lafite itself—I deliberately do not use the word 'cadet', because analogy with Mouton Cadet would be unfairly misleading. Mouton Cadet is a wine entitled only to the appellation, 'Bordeaux'. It may come from any part of the whole Bordeaux area, not even from the Médoc, to be blended at Mouton—it need not be related to the great wine of that name, either in soil or in *encèpagement*.[2]

The Carruades, on the other hand, is made from the same grapes as the Lafite itself, in the same proportions, grown in the same *vignoble*, made by the same men, in the same way, and under the same roof. Like Lafite, it is entitled to the appellation 'Pauillac'. The only difference between the Carruades and Lafite is that the Carruades is made only from those vines on the property that are not yet twelve years old, the Lafite from twelve-year-olds and older; and the men who make the wine at Lafite believe, as their predecessors did, for as long as records and memory go back, that for absolute perfection the youngest vines contributing to Lafite should be not at least seven years old, as elsewhere, but twelve. In a normal year, the Carruades constitutes about one-quarter to one-third of the total output of the estate.[3]

[2] The *régisseur* at Mouton tells me that in a good year Mouton Cadet is composed of fifteen per cent second wine of Château Mouton itself (from young vines, second or third pressings and so on); fifteen per cent from the *commune* of Pauillac and entitled to that *appellation*; and all but about ten per cent entitled to the *appellation* 'Médoc'.

But that, he says, is when they are lucky. When the Médoc wines are hard, and would take too long to mature for the quick turnover of Mouton Cadet, there can be as much as fifty per cent of St Emilion in the blend, and I know local experts who claim to detect the wines of Bourg or Blaye, or the Côtes. Hence, in any case, even if such are not included, its mere 'Bordeaux' *appellation*.

[3] For the past thirty years or so, but only in the good years (1955, 1957, 1959, 1961 and 1964, recently), there has been a third wine from the Château Lafite estate—the Moulin des Carruades, with the words 'Château Lafite' only in the smallest type at the bottom of the label, as proprietors.

This is made from young vines and second pressings, but only from the Lafite vineyards, so that it is always entitled to the 'Pauillac' *appellation*: if it is not up to the requirements of that appellation it is not made as Moulin des Carruades but goes to the *vendangeurs* at vintage time, to the Pauillac co-operative, or to the distillers.

Moulin des Carruades is only château-bottled, and the firm of Nicolas has it as a monopoly on condition that it is not sold outside France, lest the prestige of Lafite be compromised. It usually fetches about the same price as such fourth and fifth growths as Château Lynch Bages and Château La

There have been rare occasions when the Carruades, though not even a *cru classé*, has been pretty well up to the standard of Lafite itself: the wine of 1950 was one such, when the yield at Lafite as a whole was enormous, and some of the wine of the older vines had to go to the Carruades, because of the restrictions imposed by the *appellation* laws on the amount of wine allowed to be produced from each hectare.

By the highest standards—which is to say, by those of Lafite,—the Carruades lacks a little in bouquet and in alcohol, is not so long-lived, and has a higher acidity, but it shows at its best in years that are only middling for Lafite; it is always a distinguished wine; always only château-bottled; and well worth the price it now commands, which is usually that of almost any of the second growths other than Mouton.

And yet, even so, Lafite is Lafite . . . The labels permit of no misunderstanding between the top of all the first growths—the senior duke, as it were,—and its well-bred, but untitled, kinsman. Even the branded mark burned on to the wooden cases in which the Carruades is despatched shows a château less elaborate than that on the cases of Lafite (rather like the distinctions between the hotel symbols in the *Guide Michelin*); the one name is displayed in a plain rectangle, the other in a fancy-sided cartouche; and it is only the Lafite that is styled, '*Grand Vin*'.

There is nothing in the rigid French laws that govern wine-making that requires Lafite to be made only from vines that are more than twelve years old, or that prevents all the grapes from the Carruades going into Lafite.

Lafite fetches about half as much again as the price of the Carruades; there is such a demand for it that every bottle produced could be sold twice over. If the grapes of the seven-to twelve-year-old vines were included in Lafite that are at present used only for the Carruades, production of the more valuable wine would go up by about thirty per cent. Why, then, I asked

Lagune, and those who are interested can usually find it in the wine-list at the old-fashioned city restaurant Au Petit Riche, Rue Le-Peletier (just round the corner from the Rothschild bank), where they also had, as recently as the end of 1967, the 1945 Lafite, spelled wrong on the wine-list and served in a cradle instead of being decanted, but a bargain at 100 francs.

André Portet, did they still keep the Carruades separate? Could I tell the difference, I asked, if Lafite were made from *all* the vines on the estate, including the twenty-five per cent or so that were less than twelve years old?

'*You* might not,' said André Portet, 'but we should.'

9. 'Mis en Bouteilles au Château'

ACCORDING to M. André Simon, it was in 1869—Lafite's first year under Rothschild ownership—that for the first time in its history the property's *whole* vintage was château-bottled. But *parts* of the vintage had been château-bottled at Lafite in previous years—as far back, it has been suggested, as 1797.

This is if Warner Allen's assumption was correct, that the bottle of 1797 in the *caveau* at Lafite represents an attempt at the time to discover whether claret would 'ripen in bottle with the same majesty as port'—which, for twenty years or so by then, it was known that port would do. Although much of Warner Allen's detail about Lafite is incorrect—especially as to its pre-Rothschild ownership—in the chapter in his *A History of Wine* that he devotes to château-bottling, this does nevertheless seem a likely explanation of the bottle of 1797, and it is possible that it was bottled at the château, and not in the cellar of a Bordeaux shipper.

On the other hand, it is thanks to Warner Allen's own researches in Nathaniel Johnston's letter books of 1799–1809 that we know that that outstanding figure in the history of the

Bordeaux wine trade was deeply interested at this time in the possibility of maturing fine claret, unblended, and unfortified by Hermitage, in bottles. He bottled some 'neat Lafitte' 1798 for himself, along with some Rausan, and by 1801 was already satisfied enough with his experiments (although he had had only a year or so's bottle-age to go on), and successful enough in convincing his customers of the value of doing so, for in that year the letter book records his first order for claret not in hogsheads but in bottles. It is interesting to note that by 1808 an Irish archdeacon was ordering, '60 dozen of the best Claret in bottles entirely of the first growth of Lafitte or 40 dozen of Lafitte and 20 dozen of Château Margaux, and fit for immediate use'—already, that is, with a certain amount of bottle age.

In an earlier book, *Natural Red Wines*, Warner Allen had stated that it was in 1846 that the wines of Lafite were first château-bottled,[1] and his suggestion in *A History of Wine* about the 1797 Lafite represents an unexplained change of mind. It may be that the 1797 was an isolated experiment, and that for the next half-century bottling was by the Bordeaux merchants.

In spite of both these suggested dates, it was certainly not yet usual even in the 1850s to bottle Lafite at the château, for we have Goudal writing to Scott in 1852 as though the practice of bottling even part of the crop had once been taken up and had already been dropped again: 'I have always believed that when in the old days I bottled at Lafite, with our stamp, wines for the account of Bordeaux merchants, such an operation was always in your interest, because by so doing these wines were sold in all their integrity, and I even believe (and I call your attention to this) that if all the wine bought at Lafite in barrel by Bordeaux merchants were bottled at the château, fraud would be impossible.'

Fraud there was in plenty, for Goudal writes to Scott of nearly

---

[1] He may have been following M. André Simon, who had stated in his *Vintagewise*, published in 1946, that '1846 was the first time that there was an official château-bottling at Lafite and, as far as I know, anywhere else in the Médoc'. The key word in deciding between 1797 and 1846 as the first Lafite château-bottling may well be M. André Simon's 'official'. Neither he nor Warner Allen gives any authority for 1846, and nobody now at Lafite can produce evidence to support it.

two thousand cases of claret in bottle that had been to India and back being put up for auction in Bordeaux. 'Among these cases there are some sold as Lagrange, St Julien, 1855, but [that had] been labelled Château Lafite . . . I tasted this wine: it was detestable.'

What we do know, for it can still be confirmed at the château, is that there was no château-bottling at Lafite of any vintage from that of 1885 to that of 1906. The ten years, 1876 to 1885, inclusive, were the years of the phylloxera there. Lafite suffered it later than most, and less severely than some, partly no doubt because it could afford expensive palliatives (the cure—grafting on to American root-stocks—came later still) which it had learned about from earlier victims.

Although the years 1877 and 1878 were, in fact, unexpectedly good, the period generally was a disheartening one, especially as it was followed by years of the mildew.

This is probably why the practice of château-bottling was dropped for so long. It seems to have been revived in 1907 because of the resounding scandal in England the year before over the 1890 Lafite. That year's wine was a reasonably good one, and the scandal was due to no fault either in the wine or in the commercial ethics of the people at the château, but it damaged Lafite's reputation, however unfairly, and it must have seemed an obvious way to restore it to decide on château-bottling, whether for the whole vintage or for part. (Château-bottling even of part of a vintage provides a standard by which the rest can be judged, and fraud more easily detected.)

What happened was this.

Along with other 1890 clarets, the 1890 Lafite hung fire on the Bordeaux market, probably because the 1888 and 1889 vintages had been exceptionally heavy. According to *Ridley's Wine and Spirit Trade Circular* of July 9, 1907, 'it was originally placed in the hands of Messrs Paris and Damas, of Bordeaux, on account of Messrs Rothschild. Later on, it was bottled by the firm named and a small quantity sold. As our readers know, the 1890s did not change hands with much rapidity, and the public sale of Messrs Cunliffe, Dobson and Co.'s wines, which included a large quantity of the vintage in question, did not improve matters, and the remainder of the Lafite was offered at a comparatively low price at the seat of production. This offer was not taken up, and recently Messrs Southard and Co. purchased the wines, and they have been since passed into the hands of Messrs Ehrmann Brothers.'

Messrs Ehrmann (then of the City, but now of Grafton Street, W.1., where they enjoy a justifiably high reputation) then set about advertising—notably in *The Times*, and in big circulars, boldly printed in red and blue on yellow,—the 'Sensational Sale' of 'an unprecedented purchase by any one purchaser of the whole of a Vintage in bottle': 12,100 dozen bottles of 1890 Château Lafite; 800 dozen bottles of 1890 Carruades de Château Lafite; and 400 dozen bottles of the 'second wine' of Château Lafite; at 29/6d, 27/6d, and 25/6d a dozen bottles, respectively. A halfpenny less than half-a-crown a bottle for Lafite!

In both their newspaper announcements and what we should now call their direct-mail advertising, Ehrmanns used virtually the same form of words. This was the circular:

'The Barons de Rothschild, the proprietors of the famous and unrivalled Château Lafite, did not during the greater part of the eighties, owing to then indifferent vintages, permit any bottling at the Château, but the 1890 Vintage, being of superior character, they had it bottled with full brand on Corks and held in a special cellar, small quantities only having been parted with.'

There is no doubt that, far from having (as they claimed in their circular) 'prevailed upon' the château to sell, Ehrmanns had picked up this enormous parcel very cheap, and after it had passed through a number of hands. There is equally no doubt that they sought, by skilful ambiguities, to convey the impression that this Lafite they were offering at 29/6d a dozen (the Bordeaux-bottled 1889 was on sale in London at 84s) was château-bottled, though they were careful not to say so in so many words.

Now in 1907, Frank Harris ('only a fairly nice man', as Vyvyan Holland was once told, and that is putting it mildly) was enjoying his short-lived editorship of *Vanity Fair*, which he tried to make successful by exposing abuses, or profitable by offering not to expose them, rather as that other 'only fairly nice man', Horatio Bottomley, later did with *John Bull*. Harris fell, more justifiably then in some of his crusades, upon Ehrmanns, but in doing so not only indulged himself in some sly anti-Semitism at the expense of Mr Baruch Ehrmann ('these advertising sheets of his . . . all discover the same bold Roman hand or nose . . .'), but also made some wild allegations about Lafite itself—that its vineyards had been destroyed by the phylloxera, and that it had lost its place, in consequence, among the first growths of the Médoc. He referred to the fact, as though it were detrimental, as though it were peculiar to Lafite, and as though it were being kept a secret, that its vines were now grafted, or being grafted, on to American root stock, although in fact all French vineyards had then been so grafted, or were in process of being, and as they all are now, as the only answer to the plague.

Nothing seems to have come of the libel action with which Ehrmanns threatened Harris and *Vanity Fair*. It may well be that Ehrmanns, or their lawyers, realized that, even had their case been a good one, Harris was a man of straw: there were other libel actions pending; *Vanity Fair* was about to cease publication; and it would not be long before Harris was in jail and at the end of his journalistic career.

In any case, it would have been more to the point if Lafite, rather than Ehrmanns, had taken action. Ehrmanns had certainly tried—and with some of the recipients of their circular they must have succeeded—to misrepresent the bottling of the 1890 Lafite, and how it had come into their possession, whereas the château's reputation had been damaged through no fault of its own.

All that Lafite did, though, was to decide, at the end of 1907 or early in 1908, upon château-bottling, beginning with the 1906 vintage. The London firm of Rosenheim, happily still with us, which for a period at that time enjoyed, or shared, a monopoly of Lafite, under the *abonnement* system,[2] was instrumental in making up Lafite's mind. Rosenheims pointed out, in a very

[2] The system by which a firm of shippers, or a syndicate of firms, undertook to buy a château's whole production for so many years ahead, at a price based upon a similar recent period—usually at rather above the average for that period. It was a system that aroused in shippers a great proprietorial pride, as well as a vested commercial interest, in a château's reputation.

firmly worded letter of December 9, 1907, to the manager of Lafite, not only the damage done by the Ehrmann coup, and the resultant publicity, but that for some years 'the name of Lafite has lost a little of its old reputation; that in Russia it has become a synonym for red wine, and that some pretty unscrupulous traders, not afraid of comparison with château-bottled wines, have not hesitated to sell, all over the world, wines of more than doubtful quality under this celebrated label'. And went on to make it clear that all this had been possible because unlike Latour and Margaux at this time, Lafite was not château-bottling.

It can only have been the phylloxera which, as we have seen, struck Lafite later than most, and the subsequent difficult years of grafting and replanting, as well as of having to make wine from young vines, that had held Lafite back from château-bottling. Otherwise, surely, a lawsuit that had taken place over the 1874 vintage would already have made it inevitable.

Much, if not all, of the 1874 vintage had been bought by the Bordeaux firm of Calvet. When it came to be bottled, Lafite refused to let Calvet have the branded and dated corks that the purchaser of a wine in cask is normally entitled to—so long, that is, as the wine is up to standard. The Lafite records show that the 1874 was 'very good': it is difficult to understand what was the reason for the château's refusal. Calvet took the case to court where, as Warner Allen later recorded:

'the judge decided that the owner had a perfect right to withhold the branded corks if he thought fit, but at the same time as a judge of wine himself he declared the 1874 vintage worthy of the name of Château Lafite and directed the merchant to have special bottles blown each with a lozenge on the shoulder of the bottle, carrying the name and date of the wine, to take the place of the branded corks which were forbidden to him.'

It so happens that I tasted this controversial 1874 Lafite no longer ago than November 1967, when twenty-four magnums were sold at Christie's for £25 to £45 a magnum, and two were served before the sale at a luncheon given by that hospitable firm to writers about wine.[3] The wine still offered sugar, fruit, a deep

[3] It may be of interest that on this occasion Mr Michael Broadbent, M.W., head of Christie's wine department, decanted one magnum at 12.45

middle colour, and even a residual trace of tannin: it had clearly been a sound wine in its time, and one was no nearer an explanation of Lafite's objection to granting Calvet the corks.

The curious thing is that the twenty-four magnums at Christie's, bottled by Cockburns of Leith for Lord Boyne, had a blown lozenge on the shoulder of each, carrying not, as the French judge had directed, the name of the château and the date of the vintage, but the address of the purchaser: Brancepeth Castle. What is more, they *did* have branded corks, in spite of the judgment of the French court against Calvet. Mr Alan Taylor-Restell, of Christie's wine department, believes that Cockburns must have had corks specially branded here, regardless of the château's decision in the matter, and the legal support for it.

In this case, the wine was both good and (one must suppose) authentic, and the shippers reputable, even though it looks as though they had behaved improperly in the matter of the corks. But that this sort of thing could happen was a strong reason for château-bottling and, as I have suggested, had it not been for the phylloxera and its aftermath, would almost certainly have become the rule at Lafite long before it did.

*   *   *

Lafite has been concerned with only one other lawsuit about its wine, when the 1928, the wine of a hot year, fermented for a second time, after leaving the vats, in the similarly hot summer of the following year. The wine was saved from complete ruin by pasteurization, but the brokers rejected the wine, and the courts released them from their contracts. Today, methods of vinification are such that a secondary fermentation is more than unlikely,

---

for luncheon at 1.30, on the principle that the older the wine the later it should be decanted, lest it fade. But the owner-vendor had previously registered his disagreement with this principle, and the other magnum had been decanted at 8 p.m. the previous evening. To the surprise of all of us, it was the wine that had been decanted later that was the more faded in colour and the thinner in taste and in fragrance. The other, though clearly showing its age, nevertheless still had more to offer, both in scent and in taste, and it is this that I describe above. The owner had been right and the experts wrong, but of course two other magnums might have behaved in precisely the opposite way.

but if a Lafite vintage were to prove so disappointing as the 1928 it would undoubtedly be *déclassé* and sold as Pauillac, simply.

There are arguments against château-bottling, as I indicated in chapter 7, though the first-growth châteaux are now aware of them, and Lafite, for one, certainly proposes to bottle each vintage in future in a continuous process over a much shorter period than has sometimes, even recently, as in 1967, been the case. But although château-bottling can never, of itself, guarantee quality, it always guarantees authenticity. Today, it is obligatory for every drop of wine grown at Lafite—Carruades and Moulin des Carruades included—and it could never happen now, as it did when the Rothschilds had newly taken over, and as Bertall recorded not very long after, that 'you could ask any Bordeaux wine-merchant for Laffitte, and he will see that you get it next day: but what Laffitte!'

Nowadays, though it might not be so easy as that, even in Bordeaux, to get as much Lafite as you want, of the year you want, within twenty-four hours, you can be certain, thanks to château-bottling, that what you do get is in fact Lafite.

And once you have it, all that needs to be remembered is the advice given by Baron Elie as the introduction to Miss Nancy Mitford's translation of Denise Bourdet's brochure about Lafite:

'There is a great deal of snobbish talk about the best way to treat and drink claret, but it is all great nonsense. The best way to treat and drink claret is to pull out the cork and lap it up. Claret is a pleasure, not a puzzling and dreadful duty. Do not put it in the refrigerator, do not shake it as if it were a cocktail—these are the only don'ts. Room temperature is best for red wines—a little cooler does not matter, a good deal warmer is a mistake. Should you be obliged to get a bottle out of a very cold cellar at the last minute you can take off the chill by swilling out a decanter with hot water and pouring the wine into it.

'Some people make heavy weather of wine-merchants' lists in which the different years are awarded marks of stars. Unnecessary. All good vineyards sell off the products of a poor year as ordinary wine—anything "château-bottled" is fit to drink. The wine trade, like all trades, has a jargon of its own; when wine-growers speak of a good year they only mean a year that has produced a vintage that will improve by keeping. A "great" year produces a wine that should not be drunk until twenty years later. The wine-merchants give two stars to Château Lafite 1952, and yet it is better now[4] than the 1949, with five stars, which is still too young.

'Use your own judgement, above all humour your own taste—you are the person to decide what, for you, is the best wine.'

But Baron Elie knew, when he wrote that, that for so many of us it is Lafite.

[4] This was written in 1960.

Appendix 1: Annual Yields

THIS is the summary record kept by successive *régisseurs* at Lafite of the quantity and quality of each year's yield, along with the date at which the vintage opened. No records remain of the period before 1847.

Many more details are, of course, on record, from the dates at which the vines flowered to the day-to-day progress of vinification, but to have reprinted them all would, I think, have made the book burdensome, in more senses than one, to the general reader.

The notes on quantity and quality seemed to me to be terse and simple enough not to need translation from the original French.

Year	Opening date of vintage	Quantity	Quality	Product of Lafite (including Carruades) in tonneaux*
1847	25 Septembre	Très abondante	Exquis, pas très corsés	150
1848	20 Septembre	Très abondante	Exquis, corsés	100
1849	22 Septembre	Moyenne	Ordinaire	98
1850	29 Septembre	Abondante	Très légers, ordinaires	110
1851	27 Septembre	Moyenne	Bons corsés	95
1852	24 Septembre	Moyenne	Très légers, assez bons	100
1853	9 Octobre	Très minime	Très mauvaise	45
1854	6 Octobre	Très minime à cause de l'oïdium	Entachés d'un goût d'oïdium	22
1855	7 Octobre	Très minime à cause de l'oïdium	Passable	60

* In Bordeaux a *tonneau* is a measure, not an actual cask. It represents four Bordeaux *barriques*, each of which yields 24 cases of 12 bottles each.

Year	Opening date of vintage	Quantity	Quality	Product of Lafite (including Carruades) in tonneaux
1856	1 Octobre	Très peu abondante à cause de l'oïdium	Très médiocres, jugés bons d'abord et payés très chers	50
1857	20 Septembre	Peu abondante	Ordinaire	90
1858	20 Septembre	Assez abondante	Très bons, corsés	150
1859	23 Septembre	Peu abondante	Ordinaire, vins entachés du gout d'oïdium	55
1860	26 Septembre	Abondante	Très légers et très mauvais	170
1861	22 Septembre	Très minime, à cause de la grande gelée du 6 Mai	Bons, élégants, payés très chers	100
1862	20 Septembre	Assez abondante	Qualité moyenne	75
1863	23 Septembre	Peu abondante	Qualité passable, mais manquant de maturité	58
1864	17 Septembre	Très abondante	Exquis, extraordinairement moëlleux, mûrs, bouquetés et séveux (vins complets)	160
1865	6 Septembre	Très abondante	Bons et mûrs, mais durs ont été très longs à se faire	195
1866	21 Septembre	Moyenne	Très mauvais	208
1867	18 Septembre	Peu abondante	Ordinaire	69
1868	7 Septembre	Assez abondante	Gros vins, durs sans charme, payés fort chers	100
1869	15 Septembre	Très abondante	Remarquables et complets	170
1870	10 Septembre	Assez abondante	Très bons, très murs, très corsés	189
1871	18 Septembre	Assez abondante	Légers mais très élégants	153

Year	Opening date of vintage	Quantity	Quality	Product of Lafite (including Carruades) in tonneaux
1872	22 Septembre	Peu abondante	Ordinaire	130
1873	20 Septembre	Peu abondante	Ordinaire, gelée terrible le 28 Avril	116
1874	14 Septembre	Très abondante	Très bons	247
1875	24 Septembre	Très abondante	Très bons et élégants	246
1876*	26 Septembre	Peu abondante	Très ordinaires	87
1877*	20 Septembre	Assez abondante	Année légère, mais vins charmants	190
1878*	19 Septembre	Assez abondante	Très bonne	177
1879*	9 Octobre	Peu abondante	Ordinaire	87
1880*	21 Septembre	Peu abondante	Ordinaire	97
1881*	12 Septembre	Peu abondante	Vins solides, mais sans charme	104
1882*	28 Septembre	Moyenne	Très légers, assez élégants, entachés de mildew	110
1883*	27 Septembre	Moyenne	Légers, qualité très ordinaire	170
1884*	25 Septembre	Deux tiers de récolte	Vins médiocres, mildew	97
1885*	29 Septembre	Demi récolte	Qualité très ordinaire entachée de mildew	69
1886	25 Septembre	Deux tiers de récolte	Qualité ordinaire, très affectée par le mildew	121
1887	19 Septembre	Demi récolte	Vins corsés et sains, grâce aux traitements contre le mildew	120
1888	2 Octobre	Abondante	Bonne, élégante	224
1889	29 Septembre	Abondante	Convenable, assez élégants	204
1890	29 Septembre	Moyenne	Vins corsés, colorés assez bons	143
1891	2 Octobre	Moyenne	Vins médiocres et verts	147
1892	22 Septembre	Demi récolte	Coup de siroco le 15 Août 43°, vins échaudés et sans couleur, élégants	67

* These were the years of the phylloxera at Lafite.

133

Year	Opening date of vintage	Quantity	Quality	Product of Lafite (including Carruades) in tonneaux
1893	15 *Août*	*Abondance exceptionelle*	*Les vendanges commencent le 15 Août, les vins qu'on avait crû excellents donnèrent de fortes déceptions*	210
1894	5 *Octobre*	*Demi récolte*	*Vins sans qualité, verts et maigres*	150
1895	22 *Septembre*	*Moyenne*	*Année de très grosse chaleur. Beaucoup de vins piquent. Les vins sauvés furent remarquables*	99
1896	20 *Septembre*	*Très abondante*	*Vins fins et délicats*	192
1897	20 *Septembre*	*Demi récolte*	*Vins très médiocres*	62
1898	23 *Septembre*	*Demi récolte*	*Vins un peu durs, mais qui furent appréciés sur le tard*	120
1899	24 *Septembre*	*Abondante*	*Année de très grande qualité*	145
1900	24 *Septembre*	*Très abondante*	*Année de très grande qualité*	213
1901	15 *Septembre*	*Très abondante*	*Vins minces qui se vendirent pour rien. Certains crûs tournèrent fort plaisamment*	184
1902	27 *Septembre*	*Abondante*	*Très ordinaire*	143
1903	28 *Septembre*	*Abondante*	*Insignifiante, très médiocre*	134
1904	19 *Septembre*	*Abondante*	*Bons, sans être d'une qualité exceptionnelle, ont déçu en vieillissant*	150
1905	18 *Septembre*	*Abondante*	*Légers, mais très élégants*	168
1906	17 *Septembre*	*Demi récolte*	*Vins exceptionnellement corsés et de grande qualité*	137
1907	25 *Septembre*	*Abondante*	*Légers, élégants ressemblant aux 1905*	173
1908	21 *Septembre*	*Moyenne*	*Un peu durs sans charme*	116
1909	26 *Septembre*	*Moyenne*	*Légers, qualité très ordinaire, on les croyait bons à l'origine*	100

Appendix I: Annual Yields

Year	Opening date of vintage	Quanity	Quality	Product of Lafite (including Carruades) in tonneaux
1910	10 Octobre	1/4 récolte	Très mauvais	38
1911	20 Septembre	Moyenne	Année de très forte chaleur, bons vins	52
1912	26 Septembre	Abondante	Vins médiocres & maladifs	118
1913	25 Septembre	Abondante	Vines médiocres & maladifs	114
1914	20 Septembre	Moyenne	Les vins qu'on avait crû très bons donnèrent de grandes déceptions	90
1915	22 Septembre	Demi récolte	Mauvaise	30
1916	26 Septembre	Moyenne	Vins solides et corsés manquant un peu de charme	130
1917	19 Septembre	Moyenne	Vins légers et bouquetés	62
1918	24 Septembre	Moyenne	Vins sains mais crus	140
1919	24 Septembre	Abondante	Vins légers sans grande qualité	123
1920	22 Septembre	Moyenne	Très bonne année	63
1921	15 Septembre	Moyenne	Année extrêmement chaude, difficiles à soigner ressemblant aux 1895, mais de très grande qualité	131
1922	19 Septembre	Abondance exceptionnelle	Vins légers et plats, sans grande qualité	175
1923	1 October	Moyenne	Un peu échaudés, sans beaucoup de couleur, mais beaucoup de charme	80
1924	19 Septembre	Abondante	Bonne année	160
1925	3 Octobre	Abondante	Vins verts, manquant de maturité	225
1926	4 Octobre	Demi récolte	Très bonne année	40
1927	27 Septembre	Moyenne	Mauvaise	80
1928	25 Septembre	Moyenne	Excellente année. Vins gros et mûrs, un peu durs	150

Year	Opening date of vintage	Quantity	Quality	Product of Lafite (including Carruades) in tonneaux
1929	26 *Septembre*	*Moyenne*	*Qualité exceptionnelle, la meilleure année depuis 1900*	150
1930	1 *Octobre*	*Demi récolte*	*Mauvaise*	90
1931	25 *Septembre*	*Moyenne*	*Médiocre*	125
1932	15 *Octobre*	*Demi récolte*	*Qualité exécrable*	115
1933	22 *Septembre*	*Moyenne*	*Vins légers et bouquetés*	110
1934	14 *Septembre*	*Abondante*	*Bonne année vins sains et vigoureux*	190
1935	30 *Septembre*	*Abondante*	*Vins verts manquant de maturité*	100
1936	1 au 4 *Octobre*	*Moyenne*	*Vins verts manquant de maturité*	72
1937	20 *Septembre*	*Moyenne*	*Bons vins un peu durs se font lentement*	112
1938	28 *Septembre*	*Moyenne*	*Vins utiles sans grande qualité*	95
1939	2 *Octobre*	*Très abondante*	*Vins légers et bouquetés*	170
1940	26 *Septembre*	*Moyenne*	*Vins médiocres*	80
1941	3 *Octobre*	*Moyenne*	*Vins médiocres*	70
1942	19 *Septembre*	*Moyenne*	*Bonne année*	52
1943	19 *Septembre*	*Moyenne*	*Bons vins quelques très grandes réussites*	112
1944	27 *Septembre*	*Moyenne*	*Vins légers ont mieux tournés qu'on ne pensait*	135
1945	13 *Septembre*	*Demi récolte*	*Très bons vins, corsés sans être trop durs. Gelée désastreuse le 2 Mai*	90
1946	30 *Septembre*	*Moyenne*	*Vine verts manquant de maturité*	81
1947	19 *Septembre*	*Moyenne*	*Très bonne année. Vins pleins de charme*	107
1948	27–30 *Septembre*	*Moyenne*	*Bons vins sans très grande qualité*	163

Year	Opening date of vintage	Quantity	Quality	Product Lafite (including Carruades) in tonneaux
1949	27 *Septembre*	*Moyenne*	*Très bonne année ressemblant aux 1947*	104
1950	23 *Septembre*	*Abondante*	*Vins légers et agréables*	247
1951	9 *Octobre*	*Moyenne*	*Médiocres*	153
1952	17 *Septembre*	*Moyenne*	*Bonne année*	219
1953	1 *Octobre*	*Moyenne*	*Trés bons vins*	202
1954	10 *Octobre*	*Moyenne*	*Vins sains, mais manquant de maturité*	171
1955	29 *Septembre*	*Moyenne*	*Très bons vins*	236
1956	14 *Octobre*	*1/4 de récolte*	*Le vignoble girondin a été ravagé par les terribles gelées de Février. Vins médiocres*	134
1957	4 *Octobre*	*Peu abondante*	*Le vignoble se ressent encore du désastre de 1956. Bons vins utiles*	116
1958	9 *Octobre*	*Moyenne*	*Vins légers, bouquetés*	154
1959	23 *Septembre*	*Moyenne*	*Très grands vins*	158
1960	23 *Septembre*	*Abondante*	*Vins très agréables*	208
1961	27 *Septembre*	*Très faible*	*Vins exceptionnels*	121
1962	10 *Octobre*	*Abondante*	*Trés bonne année*	218
1963	10 *Octobre*	*Peu abondante*	*Vins très légers*	192
1964	28 *Septembre*	*Très abondante*	*Très bons vins*	318
1965	8 *Octobre*	*Peu abondante*	*Vins très légers*	204
1966	6 *Octobre*	*Très abondante*	*Très bons vins*	323
1967	3 *Octobre*	*Très abondante*	*Très bons vins*	335

Appendix II:

Comparative Prices

In the world we live in, prestige—the prestige, at any rate, of foods and fine wines—is measured in cash.

We have seen how, ever since the eighteenth century, the classification of the top clarets has depended on the prices that they could command on the open market.

In our own time, rivalry between clarets of the same category has expressed itself in the keenness with which each great château has tried to beat the others with the opening price for each vintage. This has been especially true of the four first growths and Mouton-Rothschild.

Because of Lafite's claim to be first of the first growths, and because so much has been said and written of the opening prices that it has reached in post-war years—and of the counter-claims by other châteaux—I had intended to print as an appendix to this book a chart showing the opening prices on the Bordeaux market in recent years of the five top wines: Lafite, Margaux, Latour, Haut Brion and Mouton.

It was not until I had spent many weeks in Bordeaux, questioning *courtiers* and *négociants* about the opening prices per *tonneau* that I realized how misleading it would be to quote these figures—misleading to the reader and unfair to the châteaux themselves, both to Lafite and to its rivals.

There is a great deal of jockeying for position each year when the wines are first on offer: one château will hold back until another has declared its hand, for instance, so that it can offer at a higher price. But it is not unknown for the wine then to be bought back, once the publicity has been gained.

Then there are package deals, by which a château will sell its first wine at a very high price, again for reasons of publicity, but on the understanding that it also throws in other wines at bargain prices. And there are other deals that nobody but a Bordelais would understand—and a Bordelais whose family had been in the wine trade for generations, at that.

What it amounts to is that opening prices per *tonneau* can be accepted as guides to prestige only with many reservations. In any case, the very fact that they are opening prices means that they leave margins for bargaining, for adjustment, and for speculation. Later prices can be more revealing. But at what precise point does one compare the various growths?

It was gradually borne in upon me during my enquiries in Bordeaux that what was most helpful and least misleading was to compare the wholesale prices per bottle of a range of vintages still available. By the time these are listed, the dust of the opening skirmishes has settled and the bargains have been concluded: here we are with the wines that are actually available at the prices that buyers are prepared to pay.

The list on the following page was compiled at the beginning of February 1968, by M. André Balaresque, one of Bordeaux's three or four most eminent licensed *courtiers*, the organizer of the official wine auctions there, and the *courtier* probably most highly specialist in château-bottled first growths and other fine wines: these are the prices paid for the first growths and Mouton between *négociants*, through *courtiers*, at the end of January 1968.

Far more precisely than any chart of opening prices per *tonneau*, this establishes Lafite as the first of the first growths in prestige, as measured by price,— and not through any scarcity value: it is the biggest of these five growths both in its area under vines and in production, as will be seen from the following table:

	Hectares under vines	Average annual production in *tonneaux*
LAFITE	80	180
MARGAUX	60	150
LATOUR	45	100
HAUT BRION	40	100
MOUTON-ROTHSCHILD	70	75

A *hectare* is approximately two and a half acres.

The Bordeaux *tonneau* consists of four barrels, or approximately ninety-six cases of a dozen bottles each.

The figures I give for production are taken from the latest edition (1949) of Cocks et Feret: *Bordeaux et ses Vins*. I do not believe that average production is much higher now than then, though that of Mouton may be up a little:

Prices for '1er Crus Classés en 1855 et Mouton-Rothschild' quoted by A. Balaresque, courtier assermenté, Bordeaux, at end of January 1968:

	1953	1955	1956	1957	1958	1959	1960	1961	1962	1963	1964
LAFITE	80	70	20	40	26	75	22	60	27·50	13	34
MARGAUX	50		18	30	20		15·50	45	25·50	12·50	28
LATOUR	42		12	26	20	45	18	50	27	11·25	26
HAUT BRION			19	32	21		16·50	45	25·50	12·50	26
MOUTON-ROTHSCHILD		60	20	36	22	45	19	50	27·50	13	29

the figure here seems low for the area under vines. The figures in M. Alexis Lichine's and Mr Frank Schoonmaker's encyclopaedias, both published in 1967, bear no relation either to each other (Mr Schoonmaker's figure for Haut Brion, for instance, is more than twice M. Lichine's!) or to probabilities. Those given here refer, of course, only to the château wines themselves, and do not include such wines as the Carruades de Château Lafite; Mouton Cadet; or the Pavillon Blanc or Pavillon Rouge of Château Margaux.

Blank spaces in M. Balaresque's price list indicate either that there was no demand or no supply of the particular wine in the period under review. But I have seen earlier lists, for the last months of 1967, and in none of them does any wine of any year command a higher price than the corresponding Lafite. Nor does it in this, the latest list available before the printing of this book, and in only three of the eleven vintages is any wine bracketed equal: the Mouton 1956, 1962 and 1963. These are also the poorest years of the eleven represented. In all the other vintages, Mouton was always second to Lafite and ahead of the others, save that the 1961 and 1964 Latour was bracketed equal second.

It is also worth recording here, perhaps, those prices reached at Christie's wine sales during 1967 of those recent vintages where direct comparison is possible. (The 1874 Latour fetched twice as much as the 1874 Lafite, but this was because there was especially keen bidding from Harveys of Bristol, now part-owners of Latour, who wanted it badly, as it was a year not represented in their 'library'.)

In 1967, then, the following prices were paid at Christie's for the 1945 wines:

LAFITE	1250 to 2000	shillings a dozen		
MARGAUX	1150	„	„	„
LATOUR	1050 to 1500	„	„	„
HAUT BRION	920 to 1300	„	„	„
MOUTON-ROTHSCHILD	1120 to 2000	„	„	„

and for the 1947:

LAFITE	1300	shillings a dozen		
MARGAUX	1550	„	„	„
MOUTON-ROTHSCHILD	1020 to 1100	„	„	„

Thus, among the 1945s no growth surpassed Lafite, and only Mouton (again) equalled it; among the 1947s Mouton did not equal Lafite, but the Margaux surpassed it. The 1947 Margaux is already legendary. (The 1947 Cheval Blanc is even more so, and outranked them all at auction, but that is a St Emilion, and outside the range of these comparisons.)

Appendix III:

Where to find old Lafite

GENERALLY speaking, the French drink their red wines younger than the English do, and because they prefer to. I am not referring to those wines that are drunk within a year of their making, and made to be so drunk—the Beaujolais *de l'année*, for instance, of the Paris *bistro*—but to the great classics of Bordeaux and of Burgundy, which a Frenchman might well choose rather crisp and firm, still with a taste of their tannin, where an Englishman of similar experience and connoisseurship would prefer wines of the same breed but older enough to be fuller and softer, a little brown at the edge.

Neither is right; neither is wrong. It is a matter of taste, but personal taste here follows national differences, and is interestingly paralleled in the matter of meat: very generally speaking, Frenchmen like not only their beefsteaks but their mutton underdone (what the Americans call 'rare', and I wish the English would not), while the English prefer it well-done or only very slightly pink.

The English like old champagne, too, which the French think very odd indeed.

I have before me a list of those dinners and luncheons given by the French Government, the President of the Republic, or the French ambassador in London to foreign potentates and such, from 1956 to 1967 inclusive, at which Lafite was served. The food would certainly have been better than at any comparable British table: the wine was as certainly younger. Both would have been chosen with equal care, so the age at which the wine was served is an indication of French taste in the higher reaches of gastronomic appreciation. And if older wines had been wanted they could have been found.

For instance, Lafite 1945, which as recently as 1967 I found still hard and unready, was being served as long ago as 1956 and 1958. The last year in which it was served on a state occasion was 1959, when it was already giving place to the 1949 Lafite. (In 1959 President Eisenhower had them both, but on different occasions.)

Throughout 1960, the 1949 and the 1953 Lafite were being served—Mr Khrushchev got the 1953 during his stay at Rambouillet—and by 1961 both were yielding to the 1955, which had a pretty long run, though the 1957 made its first appearance as early as 1962, not appearing again until 1964, and giving what seems to have been its farewell performance in May 1967, since when only the 1959 has been served.

All the same, in spite of this official seal of approval on a French taste for fine claret of about seven to ten years old, when by English (and, I think, American) standards it cannot have reached its peak, there are some French-men who do appreciate, or even actually prefer older wines, as well as those who wish occasionally to tackle a museum-piece of a bottle, whether for reasons of scholarship or of snobbery.

I think, though, that it is as much the demands of visiting British and American claret-lovers as the taste of relatively few French connoisseurs that makes it a matter of pride to some restaurants in France to keep a fine list of old wines—to seek out rarities at sales, and to put away fine recent vintages in order to maintain such lists in the future.

However that may be, there are more French restaurants with old clarets than I had expected to find when I set about compiling this brief note on where the amateur may still hope to be able to drink historic or, at any rate, adequately aged bottles of Lafite—bottles, that is, of vintages earlier than 1953.

That same amateur should remember, incidentally, that 'adequately aged' is one thing, 'historic' another. Anything older than, say, a 1945 may well prove a disappointing drink—as a drink. Which does not mean that it is not a great experience, or that tasting it and remembering it may not be a con-tribution to one's knowledge of wine.

The list is of restaurants—hardly any wine-merchant can afford to hang on indefinitely to expensive wines—and it is arbitrary and far from exhaustive: there may well be small places with remarkable wine-lists that one has not heard about, and there are other places that one has heard about but that will not answer letters, or that reply that they prefer to keep their few treasures for their old customers.

But I hope that it will be helpful to some of my readers who have not been rich enough to collect or lucky enough to inherit the classic earlier vintages. It they do decide to patronize one or other of the restaurants mentioned here it would be wise, if possible, to consult the *sommelier* beforehand, and to take his advice on when to have the wine decanted—even those wines that are so old as to need decanting only at the last possible moment ought to be given some time standing upright and unopened in the room in which they are to be drunk.

The vintages available and the prices are correct as at the end of 1967: clearly, some vintages may have disappeared by the time this book is published, and it would not be unreasonable if prices had gone up by the amount of another year's interest on the capital investment they represent.

BORDEAUX. This ought to be the treasure house of fine old clarets, but the old CHAPON FIN, with its fantastic cellar, is no more, and it may be that the others have too many wine-trade visitors in hot pursuit of their best bottles to be able to keep as much old claret as they would wish.

However, that excellent restaurant, the CHÂTEAU TROMPETTE, starred in the *Guide Michelin*, in the street of the same name, just off the Allées Tourny, lists the 1923 and the 1949 Lafite at 75 and 55 francs respectively, the 1937 in half-bottles only at 25. The head waiter here is a younger brother of the André Lavanceau who until 1966 was the *chef de culture* at Lafite: he will be flattered to be asked for an old Lafite—especially the 1949, which his brother grew.

PARIS. One or two of the great restaurants of which I had high hopes proved disappointing; others have been sulky about providing information. But DROUANT (Place Gaillon, Paris 2e), two-starred in the *Guide Michelin*, has the 1945, and 1948, and the 1949 Lafite at 120, 60 and 115 francs respectively. I consider the 1948 a bargain: LASSERRE (Avenue Franklin-Roosevelt, Paris, 8e), which has the top *Guide Michelin* distinction of three stars, charges 110 francs for the 1948 Lafite, and also has the following:

> 1906 at 160 francs
> 1919 at 160   ,,
> 1934 at 170   ,,
> 1937 at 160   ,,
> 1943 at 150   ,,
> 1947 at 130   ,,

(Not all of these actually appear on the LASSERRE printed list, but in January 1968 M. Lasserre himself told me that they were available.) CHEZ MAX (Rue Castellane, Paris, 8e), also starred in the *Guide Michelin*, has the following good run of Lafite:

```
1924 at 175 francs
1928 at 175   ,,
1937 at 130   ,,
1943 at  90   ,,
1945 at 180   ,,
1947 at 140   ,,
1949 at 170   ,,
1952 at 125   ,,
```

But one of the very greatest of all restaurant lists of Lafite is undoubtedly that of the two-starred TAILLEVENT (Rue Lamennais, Paris, 8e) which includes, along with great wines from other noble châteaux, the following:

```
1806 at 700 francs
1829 at 500   ,,
1846 at 500   ,,
1865 at 500   ,,
1869 in magnums only at 600 francs per magnum
1878 at 300 francs
1886 at 280   ,,
1892 at 300   ,,
1895 at 240   ,,
1897 at 240   ,,
1898 at 220   ,,
1904 at 180   ,,
1906 at 160   ,,
1911 at 120   ,,
1914 at 120   ,,
1918 at 120   ,,
1919 at 120   ,,
1928 at 140   ,,
1929 at 140   ,,
1934 at 120   ,,
1937 at 120   ,,
1943 at  80   ,,
1945 at 120   ,,
```

A much more modest place than any of these swagger restaurants is the old-fashioned city gentleman's AU PETIT RICHE in the Rue Le-Peletier, just round the corner from the Rothschild bank in the Rue Laffitte, Paris, 9e, where they spell the 1945 Lafite wrong on their wine list, and serve it badly, but ask only 100 francs for it, and where one may also sample the Moulin des Carruades.

Some of the most renowned Paris restaurants have little or no old Lafite, but among those that I have not already mentioned, I am told that LA COUPOLE, the restaurant in the Boulevard Montparnasse (Paris, 14e) can find some interesting old bottles that are not listed, and the RELAIS PARIS-EST, at the Gare de l'Est, which has two stars in the *Guide Michelin* lists:

> 1916 at 200 francs
> 1934 at 80   ,,
> 1937 at 80   ,,
> 1947 at 160   ,,
> 1949 at 160   ,,

Eighty-five miles south of Paris, at Les Bezards, near Gien, which is on the Loire, and a good place for luncheon or to dine and sleep at if one is motoring between Paris and Bordeaux, is the AUBERGE DES TEMPLIERS, which has rooms as well as a starred restaurant, and this remarkable collection of Lafite:

> 1803 at 500 francs
> 1822 at 300   ,,
> 1861 at 260   ,,
> 1868 at 280   ,,
> 1873 at 280   ,,
> 1880 at 240   ,,
> 1883 at 260   ,,
> 1890 at 210   ,,
> 1897 at 180   ,,
> 1912 at 120   ,,
> 1918 at 90   ,,
> 1937 at 80   ,,
> 1943 at 60   ,,
> 1945 at 90   ,,
>
> and
>
> 1947 in magnums at 220 francs and in Marie-Jeannes (which are approximately three bottles—a size peculiar to Bordeaux) at 360 francs.

Near Versailles, and only twenty-five miles from Paris, at Pontchartrain, is the one-star restaurant, L'AUBERGADE, which has a list comparable in splendour (though I am surprised to see it include the 1921, which I understood to have become 'pricked'), and markedly more expensive:

> 1803 at 700 francs
> 1812 at 500 ,,
> 1822 at 400 ,,
> 1883 at 200 ,,
> 1895 at 200 ,,
> 1897 at 200 ,,
> 1918 at 100 ,,
> 1921 at 100 ,,
> 1923 at 70 ,,
> 1929 at 120 ,,
> 1947 at 120 ,,
> 1949 at 90 ,,

And, in the same district, even nearer Paris, the famous two-starred COQ HARDI at Bougival, also has a quite astonishing list of very old Lafite, more remarkable (and dearer) even than that at TAILLEVENT, which it would be worth telephoning about beforehand if the project is to drive ten miles out from Paris to dine on the terrace on a summer's evening.

> 1806 at 1000 francs
> 1854 at 800 ,,
> 1865 at 600 ,,
> 1868 at 600 ,,
> 1872 at 600 ,,
> 1877 at 400 ,,
> 1879 at 400 ,,
> 1891 at 350 ,,
> 1892 at 350 ,,
> 1896 at 350 ,,
> 1898 at 300 ,,
> 1900 at 300 ,,
> 1906 at 180 ,,
> 1908 at 180 ,,
> 1911 at 180 ,,
> 1918 at 150 ,,
> 1928 at 180 ,,

1929 at 180 francs
1934 at 120 ,, and half bottles at 60
1937 at 80 ,,
1945 at 150 ,,
1948 at 100 ,, and half bottles at 50
1949 at 150 ,, ,, ,, ,, ,, 75
1950 at 80 ,, ,, ,, ,, ,, 40
1952 at 110 ,, ,, ,, ,, ,, 55

As well as the following magnums:

1869 at 1500 francs
1928 at 360 ,,
1934 at 240 ,,
1949 at 300 ,,

LONDON. There is probably more old claret of the finest growths in England—in Britain indeed, for both Dublin and Edinburgh are the heirs to great claret-drinking traditions—than in any other country in the world, France included. But more is in private cellars than in France, and less in restaurants.

The only London restaurant I know of with a really remarkable Lafite list is THE MIRABELLE (Curzon St, W.1.) which, very properly, devotes a whole page of its otherwise distinguished wine list to:

1868 at 240 shillings
1880 at 220 ,,
1883 at 200 ,,
1890 at 180 ,,
1892 at 200 ,,
1896 at 200 ,,
1897 at 180 ,,
1902 at 145 ,,
1904 at 145 ,,
1906 at 145 ,,
1908 at 145 ,,
1912 at 145 ,,
1945 at 150 ,,

and in magnums at 300 shillings

These prices seem cheaper than those in French restaurants.

Other English restaurants with occasional examples of earlyish vintages are the UNIVERSITY ARMS HOTEL at Cambridge, where the 1945 Lafite is such a bargain at 75s a bottle that I fear that it will all be drunk before it is what some of us would regard as ready.

Down in the west country, the HORN OF PLENTY RESTAURANT, at Gulworthy, near Tavistock, has:

> 1906 at 180 shillings
> 1924 at 135   ,,
> 1949 at 120   ,,

I wish I had been able to find restaurants in Edinburgh and Dublin with wine-lists to match that of THE MIRABELLE for, as I have said, there is a claret-drinking tradition in both capitals. It is still upheld, but in private, for I have heard of no old Lafite in any Edinburgh hotel or restaurant and in Dublin nothing older than the 1952 at THE SHELBOURNE (at 52/6d) and the 1953 at THE GRESHAM (at 85s), two excellent hotels that have never in any other way disppointed me.

NEW YORK. My friend, Mr Robert J. Misch, tells me that the restaurant in the United States with the most extensive list of Lafite is the LUTÈCE, at 249 East 50th Street, New York, which in addition to every year (except 1963) from 1953 to 1964, inclusive, lists the following:

> 1890
> 1914
> 1918
> 1934
> 1945
> 1947
> 1949
> 1950
> 1952

—but the proprietor 'refuses to state prices, because "that's my business, and the price of of replacement is fantastic" '. I am told that he charges 52 dollars a bottle for the 1945, which makes his shyness of publicity understandable, but I presume that, in some way or another, prices are vouchsafed to actual consumers.

I much prefer the helpfulness and candour of the *patron* of the renowned ROUND HILL RESTAURANT at 167 Jericho Turnpike, (Route 25), Huntington, Long Island, whose cellar I have long heard good things about, and who wrote as follows:

'The following vintages are available in small quantities, and we hurry to assure you KEPT IN EXCELLENT SHAPE

1926 and 1928	(Both rather hard)	40 dollars
1934 and 1929	(Both well matured, excellent)	38 ,,
1937	(Another hard vintage)	35 ,,
1943 and 1950	(Light wines, still sound)	30 ,,
1954, 1956 and 1958	(Not great, but still sound)	19 ,,

'The following vintages are available in ample quantities—probably, at a guess, enough for the next decade:

1953, 1955 and 1959	39 dollars

Of 1953 and 1955, it can be said that they are only now able to put their best foot forward (1953 a slightly better wine). Of 1959, it is much too young, and we wish that people would not ask us for it yet.

1949 and 1945	(a very great wine)	42 dollars
1947	(very small quantities)	40 ,,

'Then, of course, we do have two excellent vintages in rather larger quantities, 1961 and 1964, neither ready for the table. As a matter of fact, . . . the 1961 vintage . . . may take a decade to reach the table kept in a cellar such as ours.'

I quote this letter almost in full because it is interesting to find confirmation of one's belief that much, if not most, of those two great vintages of Lafite, 1961 and 1964, found their way to the cellars of knowledgeable Americans, and also for the opinion of the 1959. Most experts are agreed that claret 'comes on faster' in the United States than in France or England, whatever the cellar conditions—that on the eastern seaboard it is usually a year ahead of bottles of the same vintage in Europe, and two years ahead on the Pacific coast. Yet here is a Long Island restaurant that clearly knows its clarets well, and cares deeply about them, maintaining (as we should in England) that the 1959 Lafite is 'much too young', whereas it has been served at the grandest tables of France since the early summer of 1967.

There are other New York restaurants, I know, with good claret lists, some of them as knowledgeable as they are at the ROUND HILL, but I think that, as in London, Dublin and Edinburgh, a higher proportion of finer years of Lafite than in Paris are in private cellars rather than restaurants.

There are as many Americans—and not only New Yorkers—with both the taste and the money for the finest in wine as for the finest in works of art. Indeed, it is not only for post-Impressionist and Louis Quinze furniture that American voices have been heard bidding, this past twelve months, at Christie's.

Bibliography

1. *General*

H. WARNER ALLEN, *A History of Wine*, New York 1962

DENISE BOURDET, *Lafite-Rothschild*, Paris 1963. (A pretty little brochure, charmingly illustrated, given to visitors to the château, either in the original French, or in Miss Nancy Mitford's translation. Not altogether accurate about processes, but delightfully conveys the spirit of the place, and the pride with which the wine is made)

PAUL de CASSAGNAC, *French Wines*, trans. Guy Knowles. London 1930

CH. COCKS and ED. FERET, *Bordeaux et ses Vins*, 11th edition. Bordeaux 1949. (The standard reference book of facts and figures on all the three or four thousand growths of the region. It is time it was brought up to date)

GERMAIN LAFFORGUE, *Le Vignoble Girondin*, Paris 1947. (A purely technical work, on soil, climate, viticulture, etc.)

LARMAT (ed), *Atlas de la France Vinicole: Les Vins de Bordeaux*, Paris 1949. (For the lie of the land, and the laws of *appellation*)

ALEXIS LICHINE, *Encyclopaedia of Wines and Spirits*, New York 1967. (Useful articles on Appellation d'Origine; on the Vine; on wine-making; on Bordeaux and on the Médoc. But to be read with reserve on the 1855 classification: the version he gives is incorrect and reclassification is a bee in his bonnet. Helpful on individual growths, though there are minor inaccuracies)

L. W. MARRISON, *Wines and Spirits: a Penguin Handbook*, revised edition. London 1963. (Especially useful on the chemistry of wine)

J.-R. ROGER, *The Wines of Bordeaux*, Paris 1955. English trans. London 1960. (A short factual account)

P. MORTON SHAND, *A Book of French Wines*, Penguin edition, revised by Cyril Ray. London 1964. (Especially helpful on the laws of *appellation*)

ALLAN SICHEL, *The Penguin Book of Wines*, London 1965. (Interesting on tasting, and helpful on how wine is made)

ANDRÉ SIMON, *The Noble Grapes and the Great Wines of France*, New York 1957

2. *Some Earlier Works*

BERTALL, *La Vigne*, Paris. 1878. (See note under list of illustrations)

ALFRED DANFLOU, *Les Grands Crus Bordelais*, vol I. Bordeaux 1867

JAMES L. DENMAN, *The Vine and its Fruit*, London 1875

W. FRANCK, *Traité sur les Vins du Médoc*, Bordeaux 1824

A. HENDERSON, *The History of Ancient and Modern Wines*, London 1824
CYRUS REDDING, *A History and Description of Modern Wines*, London 1833
RIBADIEU, *Les Châteaux de la Gironde*, Bordeaux 1855

3. *Famous Bottles*

The baroque period of writing about wine in England lasted from the publication of George Saintsbury's *Notes on a Cellar Book* in 1920 to the death of H. Warner Allen in 1968. This was an age in which Maurice Healy could write of Chambertin, for instance, that 'one hears the clang of armour in its depths; Mozart closes his clavecin when it is poured', and so on.

Until the war, such writers had the wines to work on: there were still pre-phylloxera clarets to be drunk, or that they remembered from their undergraduate days; most of them had the money to indulge their tastes, and the time to cultivate them; the classics provided apt quotations, and the old-established, leisured, private wine-merchants, not yet a dying race, provided appropriate bottles and scholarly companionship.

I have avoided describing in the body of this book more examples than seemed necessary or relevant of the great years of Lafite. Those of the past are no longer with us, and to read about them can be tantalizing, or even as meaningless as it is to read about great acting performances of long ago. About the wines of recent years—such as 1953, 1959, 1961—my readers can still make up their own minds, and compose their own rhapsodies. In any case, their characters are changing between the writing and the publication of these words.

But those who wish to read about the great years of the past in the fine writing of the past, in the works of men who really understood wine, and cared deeply about it, should at any rate dip into:

H. WARNER ALLEN, *The Romance of Wine*, London 1931
—, *Natural Red Wines*, London 1951
—, *A Contemplation of Wine*, London 1951
—, *Through the Wine Glass*, London 1954
C. W. BERRY, *In Search of Wine*, London 1935
IAN M. CAMPBELL, *Wayward Tendrils of the Vine*, London 1948
—, *Reminiscenses of a Vintner*, London 1950
MAURICE HEALY, *Stay Me With Flagons*, 2nd edition, annotated by Ian M. Campbell. London 1949

4. *The Rothschilds*

Lafite does not loom large in the history of the Rothschilds. The only book about the family even to mention it, and that only incidentally, is:

Bibliography

FREDERIC MORTON, *The Rothschilds, a Family Portrait*, New York and London 1963. (A bright, gossipy, and entertaining general history of the family)

Other books that give something of the character of the family in general, and of Baron James and Baroness Betty in particular, are:

IGNATIUS BALLA, *The Romance of the Rothschilds*, London 1913
LADY BATTERSEA, *Reminiscences*, London 1923
JEAN BOUVIER, *Les Rothschild*, Paris 1967
EGON CAESAR CORTI, *The Rise of the House of Rothschild*
—, *The Reign of the House of Rothschild*, trans. Lunn. London 1928
CECIL ROTH, *The Magnificent Rothschilds*, London 1939

The enigmatic figure of Ignace-Joseph Vanlerberghe, from whose heirs the Rothschilds bought Lafite, flits elusively through the pages of:

OTTO WOLFF, *Ouvrard, Speculator of Genius*, trans. Stewart Thomson. New York 1963
A. ARTHUR-LEVY, *Un Grand Profiteur du Guerre sous la Révolution, l'Empire et la Restauration: C. J. Ouvrard*, Paris 1929
M. PAYARD, *Le Financier G. J. Ouvrard, 1770–1846*, Paris 1958

but there is nothing in any of these works about his ownership of Lafite.

*   *   *

Finally, much of the background to the classification of 1855, and to the negotiations over the Paris Exhibition of 1855 and the London Exhibition of 1862, is to be found in the *Extraits des Procès-Verbaux: Lettres et Mémoires de la Chambre de Commerce de Bordeaux*, second series, vols 6 (1855), 12 (1861) and 13 (1862); at the Bibliothèque Municipale of Bordeaux.

Index